4-7-03   18.00

OVERPOPULATION

OVERPOPULATION

John Zeaman

Franklin Watts
A Division of Scholastic Inc.
New York · Toronto · London · Auckland · Sydney
Mexico City · New Delhi · Hong Kong
Danbury, Connecticut

Photographs © 2001: Archive Photos/Getty Images: 61 (Anthony Potter Collection), 24 (John Liebenberg/Reuters), 39; Network Aspen: 23 top, 23 bottom (Jeffrey Aaronson), 103 (Paul Chesley), 46 (Nicholas Devore III), 72 center (John Warden); Peter Arnold Inc.: 72 bottom (Fred Bavendam), 65 (BIOS), 72 top (Estate of Sybil Shelton), 12 (Argus Fotoarchiv), 66 (Jodi Jacobson); Photo Researchers, NY: 74 (Georg Gerster), 52 (George Holton), 80 top (NOAA), 25 (NOAA/NGDC DMSP Digital Archive/SS), 80 bottom (Robert Noonan), 91 (Anne Sager), 48 (SPL), 82; Stanford University/Dr. Paul R. Ehrlich: 55; Visuals Unlimited/Peter Holden: 16.

Graphs by Kathleen Santini

Map on p. 21 by XNR Productions

Library of Congress Cataloging-in-Publication Data

Zeaman, John.
    Overpopulation / John Zeaman.
        p.   cm.
    Includes bibliographical references and index.
    ISBN 0-531-11893-2
        1. Population—Juvenile literature. 2. Overpopulation—Juvenile literature. 3. Human ecology—Juvenile literature. [1. Overpopulation.]

HB883 .Z43 2001
363.9'1—dc21

                                                                                2001017579

©2002 Franklin Watts
A Division of Scholastic Inc.

Contents

OVERPOPULATION

CHAPTER ONE
Problem? What Problem?

Imagine a spaceship traveling through the universe. Its mission is to gather information about intelligent life on other planets. As a medium-sized greenish-blue planet comes into view, the ship's science officer gives a report:

"When last observed about two hundred orbits ago, these bipedal life forms had a rudimentary civilization—agriculture, domesticated animals, some simple machines, wind-powered travel across water—"

"Only two legs?" interrupts the captain. "Interesting. What progress have these bipedal creatures made?"

"Significant," says the science officer. "Extensive modifications to the natural world . . . elaborate systems to deliver food and other resources . . . accelerated reproductivity."

"Approximate population?" the captain asks.

"In excess of six billion. The last doubling took only thirty-nine orbits around their star."

"Technological progress?" the captain asks.

"Moderate. Computers are still primitive. Space travel has progressed no further than the planet's moon. They still rely on fossilized plant remains for most energy needs."

"How many of the bipedal life forms would you estimate this planet could support?"

"Uncertain. The planet's ecosystems are already under

9

stress . . . mass extinctions of other species are occurring . . . large areas of plant growth have been sacrificed . . . resources are being consumed faster than they can be replenished . . . there are problems in the chemistry of the atmosphere. The planet may be at or beyond capacity already."

"Prognosis?"

"Another doubling could trigger natural controls."

"Such as?"

"The usual. Epidemics, starvation, wars over resources, ecological collapse . . . There are already signs of polar ice cap melting."

"How do they perceive their predicament?" the captain asks.

"Awareness is minimal," replies the science officer. "Most are continuing on as if nothing has changed. The rest appear to have an exaggerated faith in their modest technology to solve all problems."

"Curious."

"The next fifty years will tell the story."

"Make a note in the log," the captain said, "for a follow-up observation."

A TIME LIKE NO OTHER

Just a fanciful science fiction sketch? Perhaps. But sometimes imagining yourself as a distant observer, even one from another planet, can be a way to gain perspective on problems you don't see clearly from close up.

Certainly, the growth of the human species to its position of dominance over the planet is the most important thing to have happened to the Earth since the extinction of the dinosaurs sixty-five million years ago.

For most of the previous 120,000 years (the approximate time that human beings with modern anatomy have existed), human population didn't grow significantly. Observers from outer space would have seen little change during all that time. It took until

One way to get a sense of the gathering speed of world population growth is to look at how many years it has taken to add a billion people.

Year	Population	Number of years to add a billion
1804	1 billion	120,000 years
1927	2 billion	123 years
1960	3 billion	33 years
1974	4 billion	14 years
1987	5 billion	13 years
1999	6 billion	12 years

about 1804 for the population to reach the one billion mark. But then things really took off. In just another 123 years—by 1927—population reached its second billion. It took a brief thirty-three years to add a third billion and a mere fourteen years to add a fourth. The fifth billion, reached in 1987, took only thirteen years, and the sixth billion, in 1999, took but twelve.

Can you see why there are people who say we live in a very unusual time? Not only has each billion come faster than the one before, but most of the increase has happened in the last fifty years. If you were born before 1987, the world has added more than a billion people just in your lifetime. What once took hundreds of thousands of years now happens in a mere dozen years or so. What current milestone or trend can compare to this?

THE PROBLEMS OF RAPID GROWTH

The population explosion, as it is often called, is not just an awe-inspiring numerical phenomenon. It has consequences that touch every aspect of human life. It has produced gigantic cities surrounded by sprawling shantytowns, and it has caused millions of people to migrate in hopes of a better life. It has drained resources, such as forests, water, and ocean fisheries. It has put a strain on governments and social services. It has worsened almost every environmental problem from air and water pollution to plant and animal extinctions, rainforest destruction, and, most serious of all, global warming.

The situation is worst in the poorest countries where attempts to combat problems are rendered all the more difficult by the addition of more people. Consider sub-Saharan Africa, one of the most troubled areas in the world. Malnutrition is already a serious problem there, as is the availability of fresh water. So is health care on a continent ravaged by the AIDS epidemic. And so are education and poverty in general. But the population of some African countries is expected to double and possibly even triple by the year 2050.

Children collect insects for food in sub-Saharan regions like Akon, Sudan.

Even if populations only double, those countries will need twice as much food, twice as much fresh water, twice as many homes, twice as many jobs, twice as many schools and teachers, and twice as many doctors and hospital beds. When problems multiply so fast, governments can't keep up. This can lead to political instability and increased tensions between ethnic or tribal factions. Wars or civil unrest may result, leading thousands, even millions of people, to become migrants or refugees, spreading instability in the region.

The developed nations have a different kind of problem. Their population growth has slowed, but their affluent lifestyle makes them the major consumers and polluters of the world. In a global economy where goods and resources are routinely shipped thousands of miles, the affluent countries' demand for oil, wood, meat, fish, and manufactured products is felt all over the world. The people in richer countries consume many times what those in poorer nations do. A typical American, for example, uses twenty times the energy of a Costa Rican, fifty times that of a Malagasy, and seventy times that of a Bangladeshi.

THE TABOO SUBJECT

As you read through this book, you may find yourself wondering whether population problems could really be so serious, and if they are, why you haven't heard more about them elsewhere. Most of us trust the media to warn us about big problems. If it's something really important, we expect to see headlines, cover stories on magazines, television specials—maybe even a movie. After all, even the remote possibility that a gigantic asteroid could strike the Earth sometime in the next million years or so has inspired front page stories and *two* movies.

But there are some problems that no one really wants to talk about. Back in the early 1950s, for example, it was race. Before the civil rights movement, no one wanted to talk about inequalities between blacks and whites. Newspapers didn't write about it.

People knew it was there, they knew it was a serious problem, and they knew that more should be done about it, but it was just too difficult a subject to bring up. It touched too many nerves.

Today, overpopulation is the taboo. It's an unusually controversial and emotionally charged subject that touches on some of humanity's most basic and private activities: sexual behavior, reproduction, and family life. Some consider the very question of population control to be immoral or a threat to individual freedom.

But, you may ask, even if it is controversial, how could the world ignore such a major problem?

GEESE, BEARS, AND PIGEONS . . . BUT NOT PEOPLE

How does your local newspaper cover the overpopulation subject? If you have access to its database of past articles through your own computer or one at the local library, you can do a search for the word and see how many articles turn up.

For example, using Nexis.com, a search was made of *New York Times* articles published in a single year, between May of 1999 and May of 2000. The search turned up a scant nineteen articles containing the word "overpopulation." And very few of those nineteen even dealt with the problem in a serious way. Six of the nineteen weren't even about human beings, but instead focused on animal overpopulation (deer, geese, cormorants, bears, and pigeons). Three more were letters to the editor from readers, trying to draw attention to the problem. One was a humorous article by a schoolteacher about crowded conditions on class trips. In several, the word was used only in a passing reference: a review of a National Geographic documentary, a quote by an environmentalist, and a job description in a wedding announcement.

One article briefly mentioned overpopulation as something that might concern the president on a trip to Bangladesh. Another was about a man who had put up a billboard message about immigration levels and cited overpopulation as a concern. In the only article that made overpopulation the central theme, an opinion piece, the writer's purpose was to argue that overpopulation wasn't really a problem.

Two things make this possible: One, population growth is a trend, and trends don't grab our attention the way dramatic events or single catastrophes do, even if the trend is much more significant in the long run. That's why you'll see headlines about a flood or an earthquake or even some imagined asteroid, but rarely one about population growth, unless it's a particular milestone, such as the Day of Child Six Billion in October of 1999. But population growth doesn't happen on any specific day or at any specific place. It's the outcome of moment-by-moment births and deaths in millions of different places all over the world.

Second, many people see the symptoms of overpopulation without identifying overpopulation as the cause. The observer from outer space looks down and sees that Earthlings have been multiplying rapidly. He looks more closely and sees some obvious consequences: other species are being pushed into extinction, forests are being rapidly destroyed, many people don't have enough food or water, the atmosphere is being altered, and so on.

Down here on Earth, however, people "don't connect the dots," as one environmentalist put it. For example, you can find plenty of articles in your local newspaper about water shortages, hunger, homelessness, illegal immigration, rainforest destruction, or global warming, but rarely will these articles mention overpopulation, even when it's an obvious and direct cause.

So, why is overpopulation such a sensitive subject? It runs afoul of viewpoints and prejudices across the entire spectrum of public opinion—from the political left to the political right, from "pro-life" advocates to global capitalists, from religious fundamentalists to libertarians. Even some environmentalists steer clear of the population "hot potato." Let's take a closer look at some of these objections.

RELIGIOUS OBJECTIONS

The Bible says "be fruitful and multiply," and some religions, Catholicism in particular, believe that using devices to prevent pregnancy goes against God's wishes. Hence, the Catholic Church

Pro-life demonstrators protest against abortion.

has been a major foe of international birth control programs. Abortion is an even more highly charged issue, and overpopulation suffers from guilt by association among those who call themselves "pro-life." Although abortion is not a necessary part of birth control programs—and many overpopulation activists are similarly opposed to it—many pro-lifers believe that efforts to control population will inevitably lead to more abortions.

Even putting aside the contraception and abortion issues, many religious people are simply uncomfortable with talk of overpopulation because it seems to negate their view of childbearing as inherently charitable, generous, and good.

ECONOMIC OBJECTIONS

Another set of objections comes from those who see nothing but "less" in a world of reduced population. Nations see themselves in competition with other nations, and leaders fear that a shrinking population will be one with less military or economic strength. Business leaders worry that fewer people in the world will mean fewer customers and less business. Politicians worry that fewer babies will lead to an aging or "graying" population that will lack enough young workers to support retirees, through systems such as Social Security.

POLITICAL OBJECTIONS

Even many social activists and reformers avoid the population problem. People committed to correcting inequities and unfair political systems, for example, worry that attributing social problems such as hunger, homelessness, or poverty to overpopulation takes attention away from what they consider the "real" causes of human suffering: repressive governments, and political and economic injustices.

In addition, the fact that most of the population growth today is taking place in countries where the people are non-white makes some people avoid pointing to it as "a problem," for fear that their attitude will be perceived as "racist."

MIDPOINT IN A CRISIS

We'll return to some of these issues in later chapters, but when a subject is as fraught with controversy as overpopulation is, it's important for the reader to be aware of the emotional dimension at the very outset.

During the next fifty years, the United Nations projects that the population of the world will grow from its present size of about six billion to about nine billion, and perhaps as high as twelve billion. Even if it is only nine billion, that means we are only at the midpoint of a hundred-year population explosion that began in 1950. So the population crisis is hardly over.

No one knows what a world of nine billion or twelve billion will be like. Some of the worst-case scenarios involve famines, epidemics, mass migrations, and wars sparked by fighting over fresh water and other dwindling resources. Whatever the future brings, overpopulation will likely be the biggest issue the world will face over the next fifty years. If you are in your teens or younger, that means it will be a problem that will be with you for most of your life.

One thing is clear. We can't keep pretending the giant isn't there.

CHAPTER TWO

Why This Is a Unique Time

D o we really live in a unique time? Is what's going on with population really so special? Most of us are used to hearing that we're special—ours, after all, is a time of incredible innovation—computers, routine jet travel, forays into space, atomic weapons. No one dreamed such things could be reality a hundred years ago. Isn't our big population just another undreamed of aspect of our modern world?

No, and here's why. Think of two histories. One is human history into which all of those accomplishments we just mentioned fall. Human history—the history of civilization, at least—goes back maybe ten thousand years. The other history is the history of the Earth itself. In that history, which stretches back *five billion* years, the big events are phenomena such as the hardening of the Earth's crust, the movement of the continents, the evolution of simple life forms, the celestial impact that brought on the extinction of the dinosaurs, and the evolution and spread of the human species.

Our species has done what no other species has ever done: dominate the planet. We don't just dominate the other species; we dominate the Earth itself. In so doing, we are altering the planet—changing its atmosphere, degrading its ecosystems, eliminating other species—in ways that no other animal has ever done. These changes are happening because there are suddenly six billion very busy, very hungry, and very clever humans spread out over the planet's land masses, and they are acting, not just as individuals, but as a social group, a colony with elaborate manufacturing, communication, and transportation systems.

Our intuition may tell us that our growth in numbers has been the result of a slow and gradual process, because that is how it feels to us. But our intuition is wrong. The growth and spread of the human colony has been extremely sudden and unlike anything in the past. Moreover, it is probably unlike anything that will come in the future. What does that mean? Only that it's virtually impossible for the human race to keep up this trick, to continue growing at the present rate, even for just another century. If the human race can manage to survive this incredible growth spurt and establish itself in a stable, sustainable way on the planet, then this will be looked upon as a temporary phenomenon—something akin to a flashflood or a wildfire—that will never be repeated.

GETTING A FEEL FOR THE NUMBERS

The first step in understanding what has happened is to get a feel for the numbers. Let's start with the biggest number: the population of the world. The U.S. Bureau of the Census (www.census.gov) maintains a Web page, World POPClock Projection, that updates the world population every day. As I write this book in November of 2001, the site gives the population as 6,185,441,974.

For simplicity's sake, we'll round off the number to six billion. Do you have any sense of how big six billion is? Most of us have trouble imagining numbers that are so far outside normal human experience. In our everyday lives, few of us deal with billions of anything (unless we are billionaires).

GETTING ACQUAINTED WITH SIX BILLION PEOPLE

Here's one way to help you visualize six billion people. It has been said that if you gathered everyone in the world together and made them stand shoulder to shoulder for a group picture, they would cover half the state of Rhode Island.

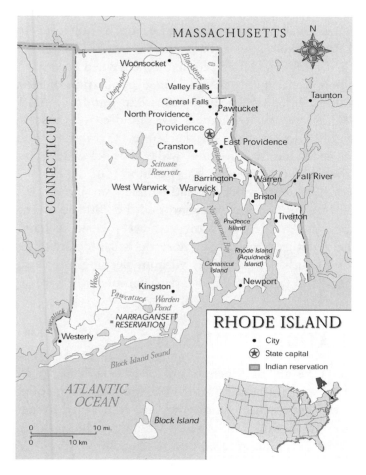

All of the world's six billion people gathered together would only cover half of Rhode Island.

Most people are surprised to hear that, because they imagine all the people in the world covering a much bigger area. Can the world really be overpopulated then? We'll get to that question later. For now, let's try to get a better feel for what six billion people standing shoulder to shoulder would look like.

Half of Rhode Island's habitable land area (excluding the rivers, lakes, and bays) is a little more than 500 square miles. A square mile has four sides of one mile each. The average person walking at a brisk pace can cover about 4 miles in an hour, so try to imagine an area that would take you a full hour to walk around. Inside each one of these squares would be twelve million people as tightly packed as people on a crowded elevator. Twelve million people is roughly the combined population of New York City (8,008,278), Los Angeles (3,694,820), and Tampa, Florida (303,447). Now, try to imagine five hundred of those squares. They would form a giant checkerboard, slightly more than 22 miles on each side. If you could walk 22 miles a day, you could walk around all the people in the world in four days.

Does 500 square miles of solid people seem like a lot? If not, imagine this: Instead of walking around the 500-square-mile people-scape, you decide you want to meet and shake hands with each one. Each greeting takes five seconds. Unfortunately, even if you shook hands night and day without sleeping or ever taking a break, it would take you 951 years to complete the job.

POPULATION BY NATION

Now let's take all these people out of Rhode Island (except the ones who live there) and put them back in their own countries so that we can get a sense of how they are distributed by nation. A whopping 1.3 billion would go to China, a billion would go to India, some 284 million would go to the United States, 209 million would be scattered among the three thousand islands of Indonesia, 168 million to Brazil, 152 million to Pakistan, and 147 million to Russia. These seven countries together account for 3.25 billion people, more than half of the world's population.

Shanghai, China, and Delhi, India: Two crowded streets from two of the most populous countries in the world.

CENSUS FIGURES

Nations find out how many people they have by making a formal count called a *census*. Censuses go all the way back to the ancient world. The Babylonians probably counted population officially by 3800 B.C., the Chinese by 3000 B.C., and the Egyptians by 2500 B.C. The United States was the first country to institute a regular census and has conducted one every ten years since 1790.

Most of the world's nations take censuses today, but they don't all do it very accurately, and sometimes certain nations wait a long time between censuses. Even with modern methods of counting people, censuses invariably miss people or even count some twice. More than this, the population of every country is constantly changing as people are born and die.

Because of all these uncertainties, there is a false sense of precision in population figures. The U.S. Census Bureau figure of 6,185,441,974, for example, sounds pinpoint accurate because it goes right down to the last 974 people. But no one can possibly know the exact number of people on Earth at any given moment.

Census surveys are taken in many countries and in many ways, such as this survey in South Africa in which the census enumerator (writing on the form) sits down and interviews the family.

When the United Nations declared that the world's six billionth child would be born on October 12, 1999, it was an estimate. The United Nations Population Division estimated the midyear total and projected that population would grow by 148 people a minute (247 births minus 99 deaths). When they calculated how many minutes it would take to cross the six billion mark, the date turned out to be October 12. In truth, no one knows exactly when the six billionth child was born or exactly how many people there are on the Earth right now—even with computers and all our sophisticated recordkeeping.

The other three billion people are divided between the remaining 221 countries or "areas" recognized by the United Nations. The smallest one is Pitcairn, a tiny South Pacific island and British protectorate which has a population of forty-seven people.

EARTH'S NIGHTTIME SPARKLE

Have you ever seen a nighttime satellite picture of the Earth? Such a picture, which is really a composite of many photographs, is the closest thing there is to a snapshot of the world's population. Although people are too small to be seen at this distance, they show their presence with electric lights, and so it is possible, in a rough way, to see where the greatest concentrations of people are. The brightest places are those you might expect: the eastern half of the United States, Western Europe, India, coastal China, Japan, and the world's big cities.

Lights rim the coastlines, rivers, and lakes. Deserts and other

This nighttime satellite photo of the U.S. is helpful because the lights show where people are more heavily concentrated.

wildernesses are inky black. We can see India's dense spray of light abruptly halted at the Himalayan Mountains. Other dark areas are the Brazilian rainforest, northern Canada, Russia's Siberia, Australia's outback, Asia's Gobi Desert, and all of Antarctica.

The nighttime satellite picture is not a completely faithful reflection of population distribution. In the less developed areas of Africa, Asia, and India, for example, people do not have as many electric lights as they do in Europe and America, and those places look less densely populated from outer space than they actually are.

MEASURING POPULATION DENSITY

Our satellite picture closely resembles what is called a *population density map*. *Population density* can also be expressed in numbers. Let's imagine for a moment that all the world's people are spread out evenly over its surface. If we did that, the population density of the entire Earth would be about 113 people per square mile or 44 people per square kilometer. (The United Nations uses square kilometers, rather than miles, as its measure of population density and this is expressed as km^2.)

Using this figure, you can see whether your own country is more or less crowded than the world average. The United States, for example, has a population density of 29 per km^2, whereas Canada, which has a huge area of nearly unoccupied land, has only 3 people per km^2. Australia, with even more open space in relation to people, has only 2 per km^2. Mexico, which is very crowded in some places, has an average density of 50 people per km^2.

China, the most populous nation, has a density of 132 people per km^2. India, the other population giant, is even more densely populated, with 304 people per km^2. Bangladesh, one of the world's most densely populated nations, has 882 people per km^2.

Many of the poorest countries are also the most densely populated, but some densely populated areas have a high standard of living, such as the Netherlands, a very small country with about 385 people per km^2.

TEN COUNTRIES OR AREAS WITH THE HIGHEST AND LOWEST POPULATION DENSITY, 1999

Country or Area	Population per km^2
Highest Population Density	
1. Macau	25,942
2. China, Hong Kong SAR[1]	6,508
3. Singapore	5,699
4. Gaza Strip	2,850
5. Malta	1,222
6. Maldives	934
7. Bahrain	894
8. Bangladesh	882
9. Barbados	626
10. Mauritius	564
Lowest Population Density	
Western Sahara	1.1
Mongolia	1.7
Namibia	2.1
Australia	2.4
Mauritania	2.5
Suriname	2.5
Iceland	2.7
Botswana	2.7
Canada	3.1
Libyan Arab Jamahiriya	3.1
WORLD	44

Source: United Nations Population Division

[1] As of July 1997, Hong Kong became a Special Administrative Region (SAR) of China. Countries or areas with 150,000 persons or more in 1995.

DEMOGRAPHICS

Census counts and measures such as population density are part of the science of *demography*. Demographers gather and study statistics about the size and distribution of populations, and about how the sexes and age groups are represented within each population. The statistics are called *demographics*.

As we saw, the population of the world is not a fixed thing. It is in a constant state of flux, owing to the steady ebb and flow of births and deaths. Demographers call these two factors the *birth rate* and the *death rate*. The birth rate is the number of people born each year for every thousand people in a given population, whereas the death rate is the number of people who die every year out of a thousand. The difference is called the *rate of natural increase*, or sometimes the *growth rate*. Another measure of births frequently used by demographers is the *fertility rate*, which is the average number of children that a woman in a population will have. Another measure of growth, or, in this case, nongrowth, is the *replacement rate*—the number of children it takes to maintain the population at the same level. This is usually slightly more than two because of infant mortality. A population being held stable has *zero population growth*.

Imagine a bucket with a hole in it. The water going into the bucket represents the births, and the water trickling out the hole is the number of deaths. If the water flows in faster than it is trickling out—that is, if there are more births than deaths—then the water in the bucket will rise. For a long time now, the number of births in the world has been exceeding the number of deaths, and that is why the world's population has been growing.

But how fast is it growing?

EXPONENTIAL GROWTH

The world currently has a growth rate of 1.3 percent. That sounds like a pretty low rate. But when the base numbers are so large, even tiny percentages translate into many millions of people. A population of six billion that is growing at 1.3 percent adds seventy-eight million people a year (more than the population of Vietnam).

This type of increase is called *exponential growth*. Exponential growth starts slowly, but after a time it suddenly picks up speed—and when it does, look out. Think of a snowball rolling down a hill and picking up more and more snow with each roll.

DOUBLING TIME

Another way to understand population growth is through *doubling time*. This means the length of time it takes for the world population to double.

As you can see, the amount of time it takes for the human population to double has been dramatically shrinking, even though the number of people required to double it keeps getting bigger and bigger. At the world's present growth rate of 1.3 percent, the world's population would double every fifty-three years, to twelve billion in 2053, twenty-four billion in 2106, and a staggering forty-eight billion in 2159.

DOUBLING TIME CHART

Date	Estimated World Population	Doubling Time
8000 B.C.	5 million	1,500 years
A.D. 1500	0.5 billion	304 years
1804	1 billion	123 years
1927	2 billion	47 years
1974	4 billion	51 years (projected)
2025	8 billion (projected)	?

THE LILY POND RIDDLE

Scientists sometimes draw on an old French riddle to illustrate the surprising acceleration of exponential growth. A pond, so the riddle goes, contains a single lily pad. Every day the number of lily pads doubles— two pads the second day, four the third, and so on. We know that it takes thirty days to cover the pond completely. The riddle then, is: "How much of the pond is covered on the twenty-ninth day?"

The answer: "Half the pond."

The point of the riddle is that people tend to underestimate the speed with which population can grow in the later stages. A person looking out over the lily pond on the twenty-ninth day would be likely to think, "Oh well, it's still only half covered. It will be a long time, before I have to do something." The person was drawing on past experience in assuming that the lily pads would continue to grow at a gradual rate. When doubling meant only a few pads, it didn't seem like much. But when half-a-pond's-worth doubles, that's a different story.

The danger is that the world's population is in a twenty-ninth-day situation.

MATHEMATICAL IMPOSSIBILITIES

How do we know that population has not always been growing at the present rate? The demographer Joel Cohen did a calculation in which he went back twelve thousand years to the end of the last ice age. Assuming, just for the sake of speculation, that there were only two people on the Earth at that time (there were considerably more) and that the population grew at a rate of 1.6 percent (the world's growth rate at the time he calculated), the Earth's population would now be about 5.3×10^{82} people.

Joel Cohen, in his book entitled *How Many People Can the Earth Support*, says, "Finding matter to construct this number of people would be a problem," says Cohen. "because the number of charged particles in the entire known universe is approximately 10^{80}, or one hundred times smaller."

Now let's project into the future. Suppose, for example, that today's population of six billion kept on growing at the rate of 1.3

percent for five hundred years. At the end of that time, the world would have nearly four trillion people. That's four with twelve zeroes after it, or 4,000,000,000,000. That means there would be 667 people for every one person today.

In "Too Many Americans," Lincoln H. Day, a demographer with a macabre sense of humor, projected the current rate of growth 6,500 years into the future. He discovered that the number of people would not only completely cover the Earth, but it would also be growing so fast that it would form "a solid sphere of live bodies expanding with a radial velocity that, neglecting relativity, would equal the velocity of light."

WORLD POPULATION GROWTH FROM YEARS 0 TO 2200

Year	Population (in billions)	Year	Population (in billions)
0	0.30	1960	3.02
1000	0.31	1970	3.70
1250	0.40	1980	4.44
1500	0.50	1990	5.27
1750	0.79	2000	6.06
1800	0.98	2010	6.79
1850	1.26	2020	7.50
1900	1.65	2030	8.11
1910	1.75	2040	8.58
1920	1.86	2050	8.91
1930	2.07	2100	9.46
1940	2.30	2150	9.75
1950	2.52	2200	10.00

Source: United Nations Population Division

This chart shows how long the world population remained in the slow-growth phase, and how the rapid growth phase has only begun very recently.

EVENTUAL STABILIZATION

Despite calculations such as these, there are people who optimistically predict that population can grow perpetually. For that to be possible, humankind must be headed for a grim world of deprivation in which the only way so many new people can be accommodated is that so many others are dying prematurely. The alternative is a science fiction world of underground cities, artificial food, and space colonies.

Fortunately, the *rate* of world population growth is slowing down. The population itself is still growing by huge numbers of people, but the slowdown allows for less pessimistic U.N. projections: 8.9 billion in 2050, 9.46 billion in 2100, 9.75 billion in 2150, and stabilizing at just above 10 billion in 2200.

The signs of braking don't mean that overpopulation problems are solved. As we will see in later chapters, some ecologists maintain that the *current* population already exceeds the long-term capacity of the Earth and that we are headed for trouble unless we *reduce* population.

It's also true that growth continues where the problems are most acute. Ninety-five percent of the projected increase will come in the developing countries. The United Nations lists sixty-four nations whose populations are expected to double before 2050. Troubled nations such as the Democratic Republic of the Congo, Niger, Somalia, Liberia, Uganda, Yemen, and the Gaza Strip will probably double in less than twenty-five years and triple by 2050. How will these already struggling countries find the resources to take care of three times as many people?

CHAPTER THREE
Plague, War, and Famine

So how, exactly, did we get into this situation? If humans with modern anatomy have been around for at least 120,000 years, why has most of the growth happened in the last few hundred years? What was going on before that?

The problem is that no one knows precisely what happened for most of those 120,000 years. There are no written records and very little archaeological evidence of early humankind's long fight for survival. Because of the power of exponential growth, however, we know there must have been such a struggle; otherwise the population explosion of today would have happened a long time ago.

For at least a hundred thousand years, Homo sapiens were hunter-gatherers who lived in loosely associated groups of families numbering a few hundred or less. Hunter-gatherer societies rarely, if ever, had population explosions. As with animal predators, their numbers remained stable, reflecting the availability of food. When there were too many, and not enough food, the weaker ones died—generally the old and the very young. Sometimes these weak ones were purposefully left behind when the group moved on. In bad times, if there were too many mouths to feed, infants were killed or left outside to die of exposure. Such acts may seem cruel to us today, but to the hunter-gatherer societies, they were necessary survival measures. Without these measures, an entire tribe could be wiped out by starvation. Whatever the conditions, one out of every two infants died during the first year of life of malnutrition, disease, or accidents.

Based on evidence and conjecture, scientists estimate that there were never more than five million people in the world during the hunting-and-gathering period. But things began to change about fourteen thousand years ago, at the end of the last ice age. The warming caused huge environmental changes with repercussions for the human species. The flooding of coastal plains dispersed herds of animals, such as gazelle, on which human hunters had depended for thousands of years. Large ice-age mammals, such as the woolly mammoth, on which the hunters had also depended, became extinct.

THE FIRST FARMERS

People changed their ways of life in the more temperate climate, and one of the changes was the development of farming. Have you ever wondered how people first learned to farm? It probably began with observations: people saw that plants grew better in sunny spots or when they received lots of water. Soon they were helping the process along in various ways—cutting down branches to provide more sun, pulling up competing plants, and, finally, planting seeds and working the soil to grow the specific plants they liked. Without the development of agriculture, people would still be living as hunter-gatherers. There would be no such thing as civilization, and no such thing as a population explosion either.

Along with agriculture came animal domestication. Cattle, goats, pigs, and chickens could be raised either for their meat or for the food they produced. Hunting became less important, and people no longer had to keep wandering to find food. As a result, they settled in one place. Villages grew up, and eventually cities emerged. Also, because agricultural harvests produce more food than could be eaten at one time, people learned to store grains and other foods and were therefore able to eat regularly throughout the year.

ANCIENT VIEWS ON OVERPOPULATION

One of the earliest known accounts of an overpopulation problem can be found in the ancient Babylonian epic poem *Atrahasis,* in which a god complains about the growing multitudes of people:

The noise of mankind has become too much for me,
With their noise I am deprived of sleep.
Let there be a pestilence (upon mankind).

And so the gods sent down a terrible pestilence, or plague. When that didn't kill enough people, the gods sent a disastrous flood. When humankind recovered from that, the gods created a demon called the "Eradicator" to continually snatch some of the newborn babies and young children.

At the time this poem was first written, about 1600 B.C., there were probably only fifty million humans on the entire planet, but people were well acquainted with the classic cycles of population growth and decline: human numbers tended to increase until crowding brought on disease, famine, or war. Infant mortality—the so-called "Eradicator"—did the rest.

In A.D. 200, the Roman Quintus Septimus Florens Tertullianus complained that the Earth was running out of wilderness: "everywhere there is a dwelling, everywhere a multitude, everywhere a government, everywhere there is life." His conclusion? "Truly, pestilence and hunger and war and flood must be considered as a remedy for nations, like a pruning back of the human race becoming excessive in numbers."

In China in 500 B.C., a man named Han Fei-Tzu complained about the hardships imposed by big families. "People at present think that five sons are not too many and each son has five sons also, and before the death of the grandfather there are already 25 descendants. Therefore, people are more, and wealth is less; they work hard and receive little."

This may very well be the first known complaint about exponential population growth.

This more settled and predictable way of life encouraged people to have bigger families. The careful reproductive habits of the nomadic hunter-gatherer were no longer necessary or even desirable: the more children a family had, the more hands there were to work in the fields.

And so, after staying relatively stable at about five million for at least a hundred thousand years, population began to rise. In 8000 B.C., when the agricultural revolution began, there were probably no more than five to ten million people in the world. By the year A.D. 1, the number had ballooned to 250 million.

Although the human population continued to grow a little faster each century, famine, disease, and war took their toll.

FAMINE

Agriculture created civilization, but at the same time dependence on agriculture put entire civilizations at risk. How? The new abundance of food encouraged rapid population growth. This stretched food supplies to the limit. Then, when crop failures occurred—due to drought, excessive rains, or soil erosion—people starved. The Bible is filled with references to such catastrophes, as are the records of other past civilizations. In a description of a famine in Rome in 436 B.C., for example, one observer told how hunger became so unbearable that thousands of starving people threw themselves into the Tiber River.

PLAGUE

The term plague is sometimes used to describe any terrible epidemic, but it more precisely refers to bubonic plague, a deadly disease that has been known for at least three thousand years. The first great *pandemic*—a worldwide epidemic—occurred around the year 500, and, by some estimates, is said to have killed an incredible 100 million people out of a total world population of 150 million.

In the calamitous fourteenth century, the plague earned the name "Black Death" because it often darkened the skin of its victims. It started a rampage that killed an estimated one-third of the population living between India and Iceland. Two new developments had created ideal conditions for the disease to spread:

(1), better transportation routes between Asia and Europe, which allowed rats carrying infected fleas to reach European cities; and, (2), crowding and unsanitary conditions within these cities.

WAR

History books tend to attribute war to religious differences, political beliefs, and the ambition of rulers, but population pressure almost always plays a big role. Sometimes a country with a swelling population tries to take land from a neighbor. Or an overpopulated country, overwhelmed by poverty and social problems, breaks out in internal fighting. In studies of aggression, psychologists have discovered that animals that are crowded too closely together become more aggressive and attack each other. Could such a mechanism operate in people as well?

Countries that are experiencing huge surges in population always have a high proportion of young people in their peak parenting years. Sending young males off to war prevents them from

THE BLACK DEATH

It usually started with headaches, nausea, aching joints, and weakness. By the third day, the lymph nodes in the groin, armpits, and neck began to swell and fever set in. As these swellings, or *buboes*, grew, the plague victim's heart struggled to circulate blood through the swollen tissues, and the arms and legs twitched convulsively. On the fifth or sixth day, the skin turned black from internal bleeding, and death quickly followed.

The frightening metamorphosis of those infected with bubonic plague, and the speed with which it killed, caused terror and hysteria wherever it struck. All normal human relationships broke down. Doctors fled cities. Signs of infection caused people to abandon not only friends and relatives, but their own spouses, and even their children.

Some people prayed, believing it was the end of the world. Others drank and partied in a last desperate attempt to make merry before death came for them.

becoming parents and therefore slows the population growth. In previous centuries, even countries that weren't involved in wars, such as Switzerland, hired out their young men to the armies of other countries. During the 1700s, Switzerland lost about a half million young men on the battlefields of Europe without ever going to war.

EUROPE'S POPULATION EXPLOSION

Between 1650 and 1850, the population of Europe soared from about five hundred million to a billion people. Why? For the simple reason that people were getting healthier. In a healthier population, fewer infants and children die, so that more people survive into the reproductive years.

What made people healthier? Better nourishment, for one thing. Improvements in crops and farming methods made food more plentiful. Plants from the New World broadened people's diets and increased the yields from the land. Among the plants brought to Europe from the New World were corn, potato, sweet potato, tomato, peanuts, squashes, pumpkin, papaya, guava, avocado, pineapple, and many kinds of beans. In addition, better transportation systems meant food could be distributed more quickly and more widely, and this further reduced the risks of famine and starvation.

The second big boost to human health came from advances in sanitation, personal hygiene, and medicine. People began to realize the benefit of clean drinking water and better waste disposal. Medical advances reduced the risks of lethal infectious epidemics. Vaccines, such as that against smallpox, were developed. With healthier living conditions, plague all but disappeared.

The third improvement in human health resulted from the higher standard of living that came with the industrial revolution. Greater wealth and prosperity meant fewer people had to do backbreaking work. People had better clothing and lived in sturdier houses. Manufactured products became widely available, as

Jonas Salk developed the vaccine for poliomyelitis (commonly known as polio), a virus that claimed the lives of many infants.

LONGER LIVES

Many people consider the extension of human *life expectancy* one of the greatest accomplishments of humankind. In 1750, the average life expectancy at birth was 25 years. Today it's 75 in the more developed countries and 63 in the less developed.

People sometimes misinterpret the meaning of the term life expectancy. When we say that the average life expectancy was 25 years old, we don't mean that people became old and decrepit at 25. A person at age 25 in 1750 might have been a little worse for wear than a 25-year-old today (the chances of having a complete set of teeth, for example, were much less) but would still have been in the prime of life. But many people didn't survive infancy or childhood, so the average of all the death ages was 25.

So far, medical science hasn't really changed the outer limits of the human life span. It remains at about 120 to 130 years. People nowadays have a greater chance of reaching that potential, but the extreme limits of the human life span haven't been extended. The best nutrition and medical care can't make a person live to be 150 or 200 years old. It can only give more people the possibility of making it to 120 or 130.

did labor-saving devices. Nowadays, when lack of exercise is a health problem in the affluent countries and people probably spend too much time indoors, we tend to forget that people in earlier centuries lost years off their lives because they did backbreaking work, were poorly clothed and fed, and had inadequate housing.

CHANGING PERCEPTIONS OF CHILDREN

By 1850, the Industrial Revolution was in full swing, and there were more than one billion people in the world. People in Europe and North America moved from rural areas to the cities, many of them seeking work in new factories. This trend, combined with lowered infant mortality, changed perceptions of children.

Although some worked in factories and contributed to family income, most city children were more dependent on their parents than rural children. Instead of helping to run the farm, they required costly schooling. Children went from being an asset to an expense.

Gradually, city people began to have smaller families. However, many poor families continued in the old ways of having many children, even when they couldn't afford to take care of them. As a result, unwanted infants and children multiplied, and were often abandoned and even murdered. In England, dead infants were commonly seen lying in the streets or on trash heaps. Foundling homes and orphanages sprang up to care for the unwanted children, but many babies and children died of malnutrition inside the homes. Concern about overpopulation led to laws making it more difficult for poor people to marry.

In time, birth rates fell in line with death rates. The average duration of life in the advanced countries doubled from less than 35 years to more than 70 years today. The number of children born per woman was reduced by half, or even more, a trend that has continued into recent decades. In the 1950s and 1960s, families in North America had about three children each. Now they have about two.

TODAY'S POPULATION EXPLOSION

At the end of World War II, the gap between the more developed parts of the world (Europe, North America, Australia, New Zealand, and Japan) and the less developed parts (everywhere else) loomed larger than ever. Not only did the rich countries have a material life that was far superior to that of the poor countries, but the people in the rich countries were healthier and lived much longer. It was as if these two parts of the world lived in totally different time periods. The poor countries were still in the pre-industrial period, with famines, epidemics, and infant mortality killing off huge numbers of people.

Acting through U.N. agencies such as the World Health Organization, the industrialized countries started an ambitious program to improve the quality of life in the poorer countries of Africa, Asia, and South America. Spraying with DDT and other insecticides dramatically reduced the incidence of diseases such as malaria and yellow fever. Public health measures produced safer water and better ways of disposing of human waste. Vaccinations drastically reduced the number of deaths due to smallpox, measles, whooping cough, neonatal tetanus, polio, and diphtheria. Antibiotics cured tuberculosis, malaria, and other diseases. When famines or epidemics threatened, the advanced countries rushed in food and medical supplies.

The programs were a phenomenal success. Death rates plummeted—population soared. Women in Africa, India, and Bangladesh continued having as many as six, seven, or eight children. Before the public health revolution, many of those children would have died before reaching the childbearing years. Now, many were growing up and having children of their own.

In only sixty years—between 1930 (when the first modern improvements were made) and 1990—the population of the developing countries more than tripled from 1.3 billion to 4.1 billion.

LOW DEATH RATES, HIGH BIRTH RATES

Although it seems obvious that a sudden drop in death rates would cause a spurt in population, no one foresaw the extent of it at the time. Why? Demographers expected that once people saw that babies weren't dying as before, they would immediately switch to having fewer children. Scientists assumed that improved health, all by itself, would *naturally bring about* lower birth rates. They refer to this kind of change as the *demographic transition*. It had happened more than a century ago to the developed nations. Why wasn't it happening now?

One obvious explanation is that the improved living conditions happened very rapidly. In Europe and North America, dis-

HOW MANY PEOPLE HAVE LIVED ON THE EARTH?

You sometimes hear it said that there are more people alive today than ever lived on the Earth. Could that be true?

No, says the Population Reference Bureau, a Washington, DC population research organization. Bureau demographer Carl Haub tells us that the rumor got started in the 1970s when someone wrote that 75 percent of the people who had ever been born were alive at that moment.

Haub set out to make a semi-scientific "guestimate" of the number of people who have ever been born. As he points out, this process involves a great deal of speculation because there are no demographic data available for 99 percent of the time humans have existed. Using very rough estimates for the number of people who lived in various civilizations at different times, and those who lived in prehistoric times going back to 50,000 B.C., Haub came up with the "guestimate" that there have been about 105 billion births since the dawn of the human race.

By that measure, only about 5.5 percent of all people ever born are alive today.

eases were conquered one at a time, and the benefits of improved sanitation were discovered gradually. Industrialization and urbanization occurred in stages, and even then family size sometimes remained stubbornly large, especially among the poor.

The modern improvements that were brought to the poorer countries of Asia, Africa, and South America, however, didn't evolve gradually. They originated from outside the cultures, and they came about practically overnight.

Also, in many countries, traditions have worked against the more practical wisdom of smaller families. In places like India, for example, people have large families so that they will be certain someone will take care of them when they are old. In other words, children are an investment in a retirement plan.

Exponential growth also played a role. There were fewer than a billion people in the world when death rates began to drop in the industrialized nations, but there were 2.5 billion when death rates were brought down in the undeveloped world. When the base population is 2.5 billion, it only takes a generation or two of large families to create a population explosion.

CHAPTER FOUR
Running Low on Supplies

When you think "overpopulation," what comes to mind? images of congested marketplaces? traffic jams? packed subway cars? We tend to think of overpopulation as simple crowding, of that feeling we get when there are too many people around us. And certainly there are cities and shantytowns in the world where conditions are like that. But space really isn't the measure of overpopulation. If you've ever looked down from an airplane, you've probably seen lots of empty spaces. From up there, it can certainly look as if there's no population problem. In fact, people who question overpopulation claims like to point out that we could take all of the world's six billion people and move them to the state of Texas and each person would have a thousand square feet—almost as much space as the average American house.

But people need more than space. They need food, water, shelter, clothing, and energy. All of these come, in one way or another, from the Earth. "From the Earth" sounds like one of those corny, meaningless phrases, so, let's consider it for a moment.

Pick something, anything, and try to figure out where it came from. Have you ever eaten a frozen waffle? Even something as seemingly "unnatural" as that has its origins in the natural world. Although it was made in a factory, the main ingredients are flour and eggs. Eggs come from chickens, a living animal that eats

Traffic jams are one of the images that spring to many people's minds when they think of overpopulation.

grain. Flour comes from wheat, and wheat comes from seed and soil and water and sun. Even if the waffle were made totally from chemicals, if we traced those chemicals back, we would come to natural sources. Humans haven't figured out how to make matter out of nothing yet, so nature is the ultimate source of everything. Hence, in order to judge whether the world is overpopulated, we need to consider not just space, but the availability of *resources*.

CARRYING CAPACITY

People's need for resources is reflected in what demographers call *carrying capacity*, a concept borrowed from biology. Carrying capacity describes how much life an environment can support. Consider a herd of deer. The number that can live in any one area is dependent not so much on pure space but on the availability of resources such as water and plants. If the deer grow too numerous, there won't be enough food to go around, and the herd will become weak and malnourished. The weaker ones will starve, fall victim to disease, or become easy prey for predators. After a certain number die off, the population will reach a level where the land can support them. Biologists refer to this as a *sustainable population*.

A little more than two hundred years ago, when the world's population was nearing one billion, a British clergyman and university professor named Thomas Malthus applied similar principles to the human population. He published a now famous essay in which he described a race between limited food supplies and expanding human numbers.

Malthus observed that human population grew "geometrically" (exponentially) but that food supplies didn't. If you gave everyone on Earth a parcel of farmland, he pointed out, the people living on that land could multiply indefinitely over the years, but the amount of food that piece of land could produce could not.

His gloomy prediction was that people would keep on reproducing until they pushed right up against the limits of the food supply. Then they would suffer a fate similar to that of the toonumerous deer: starvation, disease, and that human invention, war. They would die off until the population reached the level where people could just barely scrape by. And this is where they would stay.

The pattern that Malthus described has been played out in various places to various degrees countless times in world history. But, as his critics have been pointing out for two hundred years, his most pessimistic prediction—a perpetual state of worldwide misery—has never occurred.

Thomas Malthus, who argued that population would increase faster than food supply unless kept in check by disease, famine, and war.

USING LAND FROM A DISTANCE

Estimating carrying capacity for deer is one thing, but how do you do it for humans? Humans are much more adaptive than deer. Their social organization lets them draw on land that isn't even remotely close to them. An American may get oil from Saudi Arabia, fruit from the Caribbean, and coffee from Latin America.

These deliveries add up. It's said that the average American will, over a lifetime, consume 62,000 pounds of animal products,

55,000 pounds of plant foods, 770 tons of minerals, and the energy equivalent of 4,000 barrels of petroleum.

Now, imagine that you could assemble around you all the land needed to produce those resources. You would need some pasture to graze the animals that would produce those 62,000 pounds of milk, eggs, and meat, and some farmland to grow the 55,000 pounds of grains, fruits, and vegetables. You will need a personal oil well to pump out your 4,000 barrels of petroleum, and a small mine for your 770 tons of minerals. In addition, you would need a stand of forest for your paper and wood products and a small reservoir for your drinking water. Suddenly the amount of Earth you use doesn't seem so small after all.

In a global society, therefore, we can't really ask whether one country is exceeding the carrying capacity of its territory. There's too much sharing of resources going on. That "sharing" sounds like a good thing, except people don't share the resources of the world equally—far from it.

TWO LEVELS OF CONSUMPTION

All deer are pretty much alike in their needs and appetites. So are people, if you consider them purely from a biological standpoint. A human being that receives barely enough to stay alive is said to be living at *subsistence level* (the fate Malthus predicted for humanity). However, people don't live at subsistence level if they can avoid it. People in modern societies live many levels above subsistence. They eat more food, especially more meat, than people do in poor countries. They burn up more oil, gas, and coal, and they use up more trees and metals than poor people.

So, before we can say whether or not an area—or the world— is overpopulated, we have to take into account people's lifestyles, or their standard of living. The world's one billion richest people, for example, take 80 percent of all the resources consumed in the world. The other five billion people on Earth make do with just 20 percent. According to the United Nations, if the entire population of the Earth were to consume as much as the average Ameri-

THE NETHERLANDS FALLLACY

People who argue that the world can accommodate many more people often point to the example of the Netherlands. The Netherlands is a small country with a population density of 385 people per km^2 (that's 13 times the density of the United States and 128 times the density of Canada). Yet, it enjoys a very high standard of living. Most people have enough to eat, good housing, good jobs, leisure time, good medical care, and so on. Hence, as the overpopulation skeptics argue, we have nothing to fear from high population.

Demographers call this the "Netherlands Fallacy." They point out that the Netherlands uses roughly seventeen times more land than there is within the country for food and energy alone. The Dutch are importing, or *borrowing*, carrying capacity from someplace else.

If the rest of the world tried to live with 385 per km^2, the way the Netherlands does, there would be no extra land for anybody to import from. In other words, the Netherlands can exceed the carrying capacity of its own land only because other countries are living below the carrying capacity of theirs.

can or West European, it would take three planet Earths to supply the necessary resources.

The United States and other superconsuming countries show no signs of slowing down, but some of the developing countries, such as China, are starting to catch up. China wants to get its one billion people off their bicycles and into cars, and is rapidly building coal-burning power plants. As China grows, so does its consumption of resources. The developed countries have so far been able to live the way they do because so much of the world doesn't live that way. But what happens when they do?

OVERSHOOT

What happens when a society exceeds the carrying capacity of its land? The once-mysterious case of Easter Island may provide a sobering answer.

When European ships landed on the remote South Sea island in the 1770s, they found a puzzling situation. The island displayed signs of a developed culture, such as gigantic stone heads that stood like strange sentinels all over the treeless landscape. But the impoverished, listless tribe that lived there seemed incapable of such an engineering and artistic accomplishment. And how had the stones—some weighing 50 tons—been levered into upright positions when there were no trees from which to fashion the beams?

The mystery started to unfold only in recent years, when archaeologists began studying soil samples and sifting through digs. From this evidence they deduced that the island had been settled in about A.D. 400 by seafaring Polynesians, probably numbering about fifty to one hundred. The population remained low until about 1100 and then doubled every century until around 1400. By 1600 there were about six thousand people.

Layers of pollen from soil cores showed scientists that the island once had a thick tropical rainforest. Tools and artifacts, including the sudden appearance of weapons, told the rest of the story. For perhaps a thousand years, the people prospered and multiplied, living off the lush and fertile island's vast resources.

HOW MANY PEOPLE CAN THE EARTH SUPPORT?

In a global economy, where resources move all over the world, the carrying capacity of a specific country matters less than the carrying capacity of the entire world. So what is it? How many people can the Earth support? In 1995, demographer Joel E. Cohen reviewed every estimate ever made. The lowest estimate was less than one billion and the highest was one trillion. A Harvard University oceanographer calculated that we might have food for forty billion people. A Brown University researcher said we could continue to sustain six billion, but only if we all became vegetarians. Cohen discarded the estimates at the extreme high and low ends. The rest fell between 7.7 billion and 12 billion. That turns out to be precisely the range the United Nations predicts we will reach by the middle of the next century.

Did the original inhabitants of Easter Island go through a catastrophic population decline from using up too many resources in too short a period of time?

But as their population grew, they gradually used up the resources. They cut down trees for firewood and to build canoes, houses, and levering beams. They used the cleared land to grow crops, so that the forest gradually shrank and finally disappeared entirely. When the sources of wood disappeared, the people couldn't make boats for fishing. Erosion caused by deforestation diminished the amount of available farmland. Fights developed over land and over the limited fresh water. A shrinking food supply and perhaps some natural event such as a drought may have triggered a famine and a resulting panic. The competition for the remaining farmland or water grew into full-scale warfare. The island's economy collapsed and the population began a long decline. This was the society the Europeans found in the late eighteenth century.

Author William Catton coined the term "overshoot" to describe what happened on Easter Island. Overshooting is like writing checks for more money than you have in the bank. The Easter Islanders, he said, exploited the resources of their island until it caught up with them. By the time they realized what was happening, it was too late. Catton and other theorists see parallels with Easter Island and what could happen to our entire planet if we aren't more careful with its resources.

RENEWABLE AND NONRENEWABLE RESOURCES

One reason to worry about resources is that some are *nonrenewable*. This means the geologic processes that form them can take anywhere from thousands to millions of years to replenish. In practical human terms, such time periods might as well be infinite. Fossil fuels, such as coal, oil, and gas, for example, are considered nonrenewable because they were formed over millions of years by decomposing plant material. Metals are also nonrenewable.

Topsoil renews itself at the rate of one inch every five thousand years. So, practically speaking, it too is nonrenewable.

Renewable resources, in contrast, are those that can be replenished in a relatively short time. Trees are said to be renewable because a forest can be replanted and, in most cases, be returned to its original state within fifty years or so. An exception to this would be a Giant Sequoia forest, because those colossal trees took three thousand to four thousand years to reach that size.

Some fresh water is renewable, and some is not. The water that comes from lakes and reservoirs is renewable because it goes through a cycle of evaporation and condensation that returns it to the Earth in a drinkable state. However, fresh water from underground aquifers renews itself very, very slowly. Empty aquifers could take hundreds, even thousands of years to refill.

The fact that we are rapidly using up some resources that will take thousands or hundreds of thousands of years to replace alarms many scientists and environmentalists. They believe we are overshooting the Earth's carrying capacity and squandering a precious inheritance. One of the most outspoken scientists has been biologist Paul Ehrlich, the best known of the modern-day Malthusians.

THE POPULATION BOMB

In 1968 Ehrlich wrote a blunt and controversial book, *The Population Bomb*. On the front of the paperback copy were the words: "While you are reading these words four people will have died from starvation. Most of them children." Unlike Malthus, Ehrlich went beyond the relationship between population and food supply and looked at the capacity of the entire planet—its ecological systems and all its resources—to support its entire population.

The book caused quite a stir. Ehrlich went on television talk shows, and the phrase "population bomb" entered the lexicon. At the time, the Earth's population was growing much faster than it is today. Women were having an average of five children instead of the present three. Ehrlich wrote: "the battle to feed all of humanity is over. In the 1970s, the world will undergo famines—hundreds of millions of people will starve to death." At the time, the population was about 3.5 billion, which Ehrlich believed was the limit. Feeding six billion people, he wrote in 1976, "is totally impossible in practice."

Of course, Ehrlich was wrong about that. In the years since he wrote of massive deaths, the death rate in the world has actually gone down, not up. He didn't anticipate the development of high-technology agriculture, or the "Green Revolution," which was brought to the less developed world in response to the very concerns that Ehrlich had raised. Now we have more than six bil-

PAUL EHRLICH

Stanford University biologist Dr. Paul Ehrlich is Bing Professor of Population Studies and Professor of Biological Sciences at Stanford University. Much of his work in biology has been with butterflies, an area of study that he found relevant to human populations. "We're all subject to exactly the same laws. Butterfly populations and human populations can only grow beyond carrying capacity for a short time."

The alarm Ehrlich sounded when he published *The Population Bomb* helped give impetus to the fledgling environmental movement, but the failure of his prediction to come true has cost him credibility with critics of overpopulation arguments. Still, Ehrlich has not broken stride. He has written more than thirty-five books, some with his wife, Anne Ehrlich, and continues to warn of the dangers of energy consumption, urban sprawl, air and water pollution, and disappearing farmland.

"Everybody understands that the population explosion is going to come to an end. What they don't know is whether it's going to come to an end primarily because we humanely limit births or because we let nature have her way and the death rate goes way up."

Dr. Paul Ehrlich, author of The Population Bomb.

lion people, and human beings overall are better fed than ever before.

But there are strong signs that the increased harvests of the Green Revolution have reached their limit, while population continues to grow. Ehrlich holds fast to his Malthusian position that humanity is courting disaster and can't expect to keep pulling new tricks out of its hat.

UNLIMITED RESOURCES?

The idea that resources are finite and should be carefully conserved seems like common sense. But not to economists such as the late Julian Simon. Simon argued that people shouldn't be worried about conserving specific resources. Why? Because, he argued, when people exhaust one resource, they either find a substitute for it or they change their technology to make use of a substitute. Hence, he argued, shortages are actually good in the long run because they force people to innovate. This confident belief that technology and human know-how can solve such problems is sometimes called *technological optimism*. The opposing view is labeled *technological skepticism*.

History has plenty of examples to support the optimists' position. For thousands of years, for example, firewood was humanity's chief fuel. Coal had been discovered, but it was hard to mine. But in 1765, just as England was beginning to run out of timber, James Watt invented the steam engine, which suddenly made it much more worthwhile to mine coal. By the time it was being put to commercial use twenty years later, the steam engine had made coal a valuable resource and people were mining it in huge quantities.

"The main fuel to speed the world's progress is the stock of human knowledge," said Simon. "And the ultimate resource is skilled, spirited, hopeful people, exerting their wills and imaginations to provide for themselves and their families."

The technological optimists believe that population and economies can continue to grow forever. They don't worry about environmental damage because they believe that technology can substitute or make up for any lost environmental services. If greenhouse gases build up in the atmosphere and cause the climate to warm, technological optimists believe that science will find a way to fix the composition of the atmosphere or will come up with various solutions so that people can continue to prosper in the new climate. If the world runs out of enough fertile farmland to grow food, technological optimists believe that science will find new ways to create food. In short, the technological optimist believes that science will always triumph and that people will continue to become more and more independent of nature.

The technological skeptics believe there are limits. They contend that the environment is humanity's essential life-support system and that technology can never adequately reproduce or substitute for it. They don't believe that people can, in any realistic time frame, learn to control the weather, or replace animals that have become extinct, or build underground cities, or find an adequate artificial substitute for the world's rainforests or coral reefs.

Hence, the skeptics don't believe that humanity should gamble that these as-yet-undeveloped technologies will bail them out of problems that they are creating today. The technological skeptics take an attitude of "better safe than sorry."

CHAPTER FIVE

Bare Necessities: Water and Food

If we wanted to know the absolute maximum number of people who could live on Earth, we would first have to figure out the minimum requirements for life—the sustenance level. What do people need just to stay alive? They need air to breathe, and they need a space to occupy. They may or may not need protection from the elements depending on the climate, but there are two things they absolutely must have: water and food.

Take one of them away for very long and death is a certainty. Without water, a person can't last much more than three days; without food, a month, maybe two. And, when you take away water or food from an entire region—as happens in droughts and famines—whole societies can be wiped out or be forced to migrate.

So, in any calculations involving population and carrying capacity, water and food are going to be at the center of the equation. In fact, many scientists view water availability as the single most critical factor in determining the population capacity of an area.

HOW MUCH WATER IS THERE?

The world has an enormous amount of water, but most of it is salty and can't be consumed. Of the remaining fresh water, much is locked up in glaciers or snow and is not easily accessible. In the end, only a tiny percentage is available for drinking. Scientists estimate that all the fresh water in the world could fit inside a cube-shaped tank measuring 95 miles on a side.

Could the world ever use up this water? No, because fresh water is constantly falling on the Earth in the form of rain. When water evaporates from the oceans, it leaves its salt behind and joins other evaporated water. All of it then comes down as fresh water. Some ends up back in the ocean, some goes into lakes and rivers, and some seeps into the ground. Even the water that people and animals consume is mostly excreted and winds up back in the cycle. So, water doesn't get used up so much as it recirculates. Scientists believe that the quantity of available fresh water has remained pretty much fixed over most of human history.

ENOUGH TO GO AROUND?

Scientists say there is enough water for everybody in the world. Problems arise because it's not distributed equally. Some parts of the world have a lot, and other parts have very little. And no region is guaranteed a stable share. That's why there's so much concern about water being pumped out of the ground. That water isn't lost from the water cycle, but once it's pumped out and gets back in the cycle, it can go anywhere.

Isn't there any way to increase the amount of fresh water? Yes. We have the technology to desalinate ocean water, and several mideastern countries do this now. But the processes are very costly in energy. So far at least, the cost of desalted water is still several times as expensive as getting fresh water to an area by other means—shipping it in tanks or running pipes. Areas can also increase their share of water by capturing more rainwater and storing it, or by recapturing and recycling water that is used.

Today, about a half billion people are experiencing chronic water shortages for all or part of the year. But within just twenty-five years, that figure will explode to three billion people, and that doesn't take into account increased demand due to global warming. Moreover, most of the current growth in population is occurring in places that are already experiencing water-related difficulties, such as Ethiopia, where population is expected to more than double from 62 million today to 136 million in 2025.

That is why some geologists are convinced that water shortages will bring the human population explosion to a halt. This is also why the World Bank has warned of the possibility of "water wars" as one country tries to get access to the water of the other.

DRAINING AQUIFERS AND RIVERS

Some chronically dry areas must import water, either through pipelines or by diverting it from rivers. After being tapped for millennia, however, some of the world's great rivers are reaching their limit. Little is left of the great Nile by the time it reaches the sea. The same is true of the Yellow River in China and the Colorado in North America.

The picture is just as bleak for the world's *aquifers*, which supply some dry areas of the world with much of their water. Aquifers are underground formations of porous rock filled with water. The Ogallala Aquifer beneath the American Great Plains, which was filled by melting glaciers at the end of the last ice age, is believed to be half empty. Farmers pump out 4 to 6 feet for every half-inch that seeps in. No one knows when it will run dry, but when it does, the effect on farming will be very much like a severe drought, but a drought that never ends. In some places, emptied aquifers have collapsed, leaving giant sinkholes. In coastal areas, salty seawater seeps into the emptied spaces.

DRY SPELLS

Droughts are part of the natural climatic cycles of the Earth, but those that last too long can cause crop failures and even famine.

In the 1930s, a decade-long drought in the American Southwest caused the Dust Bowl—so named because the dried-out soil simply blew away in enormous clouds. Another area troubled by drought is the African Sahel, a wide strip of Africa that runs along the southern fringe of the Sahara Desert, cutting through about a dozen countries including Chad, Sudan, and parts of Nigeria, Ethiopia, and Somalia. A devastating drought in the 1970s caused a famine that took 250,000 lives in the Sahel.

The dry fields surrounding this farm in Nebraska were common sights during the Dust Bowl of the 1930s.

MEGADROUGHTS

As bad as the American Dust Bowl or the drought in the Sahel might have seemed, scientists say the world's climate has often served up droughts far surpassing anything seen in the last 150 years. In the 10,000 years since the last ice age ended, there have been droughts so prolonged that they have caused the collapse of ancient civilizations. Researchers believe that is what happened about 4,200 years ago when a three-hundred-year drought caused the disintegration of the world's first empire, the Akkadians in Mesopotamia. Drought is also believed to have caused the downfall of several pre-Inca civilizations in South America and to have played a big part in the disappearance of the Mayan civilization in Central America. In fact, one reason why the Egyptian civilization may have lasted so long was that the annual flooding of the Nile continually restored the fertility of the soil and made the area less dependent on rain.

Over the past 3,500 years, drought has been the rule in California, according to scientists. Some dry periods have lasted as long as two centuries. Today's California climate is a relatively wet exception to that.

Scientists are able to "read" the weather patterns of the past by studying cores of soil and sediments that have remained undisturbed over the centuries. The study of one such core has led scientists to predict that one region of Equatorial East Africa will suffer a megadrought, possibly lasting decades, in the next fifty to one hundred years.

THE PROBLEM OF WORLD HUNGER

Some people argue that food, like water, is not so much in short supply as it is unequally distributed. The Indian economist Amartya Sen, winner of the 1998 Nobel Prize in economics, studied the Bangladesh famine of 1974. People starved, he discovered, not because there wasn't enough food but because economic conditions caused a sudden drop in income that left them unable to buy it. In studying the world food situation, Sen went on to conclude that the world was not running out of food, nor would it in the foreseeable future. "Food is much cheaper to buy today than it was in Malthus' time," he pointed out in a paper entitled "Population: Delusion and Reality."

Yet food is expensive enough, or inaccessible enough, that about a billion people don't even get enough calories just to be able to walk around. Ten million people die of malnutrition and other hunger-related causes every year, most of them infants and small children.

So the current food situation is nothing to cheer about. And if a billion people are literally immobilized from hunger today, what will happen over the next twenty-five years as another two billion people are added to the population?

EATING LOWER ON THE FOOD CHAIN

There would be more food to go around in the world if people ate plants directly rather than feeding them to animals to get meat. A study by the Alan Shawn Feinstein World Hunger Program at Brown University demonstrated that current world harvests could supply a healthy vegetarian diet to all six billion of the world's people. However, a diet in which some 15 percent of the calories are derived from animal sources—a diet more typical of South America—could feed only four billion people. A diet similar to that eaten in North America, with about 30 percent of the calories from animal sources, could be supplied to only 2.6 billion people.

The reason for this is that it takes about 16 pounds (7.3 kilograms) of grain and soybeans to get 1 pound (0.4 kg) of beef. Raising cattle also uses huge amounts of water—an incredible 2,500 gallons for every pound of beef.

THE GREEN REVOLUTION

We've seen how the Green Revolution of the 1970s increased world harvests and averted the famines predicted by Paul Ehrlich. These methods were so productive that people used terms such as "miracle rice" and "miracle wheat." Mexico, which previously had to import wheat to feed its people, became an exporter of

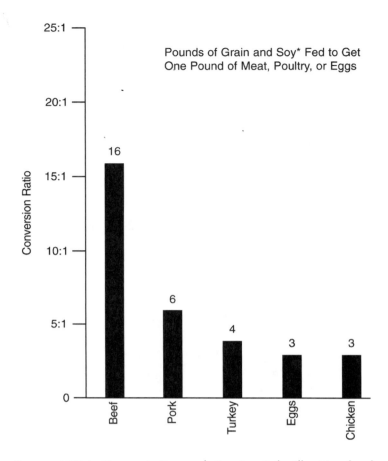

Pounds of Grain and Soy* Fed to Get
One Pound of Meat, Poultry, or Eggs

Source: USDA, Economic Research Service, Beltsville, Maryland.
*Soy constitutes only 12% of steer feed and 20–25% of poultry.

wheat. Grain harvests continued to climb until about 1984 when they leveled out. Many scientists now believe that some of the initial gains can't be sustained.

Why? High-tech agriculture is expensive, requiring lots of water, fertilizer, and heavy machinery. Not all Third World farmers can maintain it. It also takes its toll on the land. Heavy irrigation causes salts to accumulate, eventually making land unusable. Fertilizers can't continue to compensate for poor soil. In addition, cropland itself has been shrinking worldwide due to erosion and desertification, so there is less land to farm. The need to get the absolute maximum out of the soil in the developing countries has resulted in unsound practices that result in erosion. Genetic engineering of plants could increase yields, but some experts believe that, even with this advance, future increments will be small and the days of "miracle" crops may be gone.

SOIL—IT'S MORE THAN JUST DIRT

We take soil for granted. It's the stuff under our feet, right? Not always. The kind of soil that we need for growing plants is called topsoil, an upper layer of dirt that is rich in organic matter. This soil forms very slowly, and it is not found everywhere. Essentially, a desert is a place without topsoil.

Topsoil is a complete ecosystem teeming with microscopic life. Billions of tiny organisms help to move and recycle nutrients, transferring them from soil to crops. Fertilizers cannot substitute for this living system. Unfortunately, chemical and machine-intensive farming leave fertile soils depleted and vulnerable to erosion. A few inches of topsoil can take hundreds and perhaps thousands of years to produce.

Deserts like the Sahara contain no topsoil, therefore nothing can grow there.

Where does topsoil go when it erodes? Some of it washes into lakes, rivers, or the seas. When soil is used for farming, it is more exposed to the elements than soil covered by forest, shrubbery, or grasses. The simple impact of the rain scatters soil, launching particles into the air with each drop. If the land is at all sloped, more than half the soil contained in those splashes is carried downhill. Leaving crop residue, such as cornstalks, in the fields after harvest can help shield the soil. But in the developing world, where firewood is now scarce, the rural poor use the stalks for cooking fuel. When planting season arrives, dry soils simply blow away.

OCEAN FISHERIES

Fish are a major food for many people in the world. As population has risen, so has the demand for fish. This has led to overfishing—taking so many fish that there is not enough reproductive stock left to replenish them. There is probably no better example of human shortsightedness than the overfishing of the oceans.

For most of human history, people made hardly a dent in the

Overfishing is becoming a major problem as the world's demand for fish increases.

population of ocean fish. The oceans were too vast, and people didn't have the technology to seriously abuse this resource. But now they do. Bigger and bigger boats with better electronics have been efficiently hunting down more and more fish to feed the world's billions. On huge factory ships fish are caught, cleaned, and frozen or canned while the boat is still on the high seas. Whales, the Earth's largest animals, have been hunted almost to extinction by high speed boats and harpoon guns. Bluefin tuna, which are prized as sushi in Japan, are hunted using spotter airplanes that radio their locations to boats. Worldwide, fishing catches have been declining since 1989. Overfishing of cod and haddock in the North Atlantic has brought economic ruin to thousands of fishing villages between Boston and Newfoundland.

No one knows how long it will take for these fish populations to recover, and there's no guarantee that they will. Remember that population growth starts out slowly and becomes fast only when the population growth is sizable. So, if you allow the fish population to drop down too low, then you are in for a long wait as the growth gradually picks up momentum.

The oceans are a good example of how people behave with a common resource. Since no country owns the oceans, no one feels responsible for them. Or, to put it another way, no country or individual wants to exercise restraint because they think that if they don't take the fish, someone else will.

FISH FARMING

The technological solution to the depletion of the oceans is fish-farming or *aquaculture*, a practice that has been particularly successful in China. Worldwide, fish farming has quintupled since 1984, and has made up for the decline in ocean catches that began in that same year.

Its chief disadvantage is that captive fish, unlike wild ones, must be fed, just like domesticated land animals. Some are fed with grain and others with fishmeal. Nevertheless, fish farming has an advantage over meat production in that fish grow faster and gain more weight in relation to the amount of food they eat than land animals.

An even more efficient form of aquaculture is the raising of tiny shrimplike crustaceans called Daphnia. When raised in nutrient rich environments, these animals produce more food than some plant crops for a comparable amount of time and material invested.

Some analysts predict that fish farming yields will eventually exceed those of ocean catches. The continued expansion of fish farming may be a benefit to the environment, to the extent that it relieves the fishing pressure on the oceans.

THE RISKS OF BIOTECHNOLOGY

Biotechnology offers potential solutions to world hunger, but it's controversial. Most of the agricultural gains in genetic engineering have been in creating herbicide- and pesticide-resistant plants. These are less affected than ordinary plants by chemical sprays that kill weeds and bugs. So far, genetic engineering has not produced another generation of "super rice," or "miracle wheat" as was the case in the Green Revolution, and some scientists don't believe that tinkering directly with genes will produce more dramatic results in yield than does regular breeding.

Some scientists and environmental groups have pointed out a potential danger in developing plants that are herbicide resistant: they could mutate or cross-pollinate with weeds, resulting in a super-weed. Such a weed would be resistant to herbicides and would be almost impossible to stop with current technology.

Similar concerns have been raised about genetically engineered fish and livestock. By borrowing genes from various creatures and implanting them in others, scientists have created fast-growing trout and catfish, oysters that can withstand viruses, and an "enviropig," whose feces are less harmful to the environment because they contain less phosphorus.

68

A Canadian biotech company has also developed a genetically engineered salmon that grows twice as fast as normal salmon. Although the idea with animals of this type is to raise them in captivity, the enclosures in the sea, called net pens, often are broken by waves or hungry predators. Some scientists are concerned that if genetically altered fish escaped into the wild, they could interbreed with wild fish. The offspring of such matings might not survive well or be able to reproduce themselves. This could wipe out the wild salmon population.

CHAPTER SIX
Ecosystem Breakdowns

Up until now, we've been talking about the Earth as if it were a giant pantry. Is there enough water? Is there enough food? Are we running out of fish? Are we using up our forests? That's basically how Malthus saw the problem—more and more humans reaching into the Earth's pantry until they inevitably emptied it.

What Malthus didn't fully see, and why his predictions were never fully confirmed, was how different from a pantry the Earth really was. The Earth turned out to be much more like a factory— a big, buzzing factory in which all the various parts are made up of living things, all connected and interacting with one another in complex and intricate ways. Humans became very good at tinkering with the machines in that factory, adding parts here and there, and making them work more to people's advantage.

In other words, *Homo sapiens* succeeded because they made themselves less dependent on nature. It began with farming ten thousand years ago. Once people could farm, they didn't have to roam over hill and dale hoping to find the right bush with the right berries on it. They could grow their own. People chose the most useful plants (grains, fruits, and vegetables) and the most useful animals (chickens, cows, pigs, horses, sheep, and dogs), and more or less disregarded the others.

This was fine, and humans flourished. But there were two problems. One had to do with scale. As long as people made their modifications on a small scale, the Earth went on running like before. As people's numbers swelled into the billions, however, the changes began to add up. This was no longer just a few fields of wheat, a few grazing goats, and a few chimneys sending puffs of smoke into the air. Humankind had begun changing the fundamental workings of the Earth.

The Earth is made up of ecosystems. Ecosystems are complex communities of plants, animals, and microscopic organisms. A salt marsh is an ecosystem, and so is a forest or a coral reef. These ecosystems perform all kinds of essential functions that humans—and other forms of life—are dependent on.

This leads us to the second problem. The better humans became at tinkering with nature, the more they created an illusion of an artificial world. People surrounded themselves with their own inventions and manufactured products. They relied more and more on their own systems to supply their needs. Hardly anyone remembered where things such as the frozen waffle actually came from. It was easy to forget that all these artificial systems were built *on top of* nature's underlying systems.

Now these two trends have converged in a dangerous way. Just at the moment when humans have become so plentiful as to do real damage to the Earth, their awareness of the natural world's importance has dulled. Humans have changed the content of the atmosphere; the balance of life in the ocean; the distribution of forests, grasslands, and deserts; the number of other creatures that live in the world and where some of these creatures live. Because of human actions, some scientists believe that about thirty thousand other species of animals and plants are being pushed into oblivion every year.

THE POPULATION CONNECTION

Mistreatment of the environment is an age-old problem. Some early societies abused their ecosystems and brought on their own collapse. The early Sumerian culture of the Tigris and Euphrates valleys may have faded because its irrigation systems degraded the

Salt marshes, forests, and coral reefs are all types of ecosystems.

soil. In ancient Greece, Plato warned his contemporaries not to cut down so many trees or let goat herds overgraze, but his advice went unheeded. Greece today is nearly a desert, its soils thin and poor, and the vast majority of its original forests long vanished.

Unlike the ancient people who could only damage a small part of the world, today humans have the technology and the population to cause ecosystem damage on a worldwide basis. All of humanity shares the same atmosphere, so that carbon dioxide that is pumped into the sky in the United States can ultimately affect the weather in India. The oceans are another "commons." If North Americans hunt codfish to near extinction, the loss is not just theirs. If Brazilians cut down the rainforest, it has impact on the future and quality of human life everywhere.

Let's take a closer look at five global environmental problems that are closely connected to population growth: deforestation, animal extinction, exotic invasions, global warming, and coral reef destruction.

DEFORESTATION

The forests of the Earth absorb carbon dioxide and produce oxygen; they anchor soils and prevent erosion, and they regulate water flow and protect watersheds. Tropical rainforests, such as those that cover the Amazon basin of South America, capture and recycle prodigious quantities of water. Trees provide habitat for more than 50 percent of the world's plant and animal species.

People have been felling trees and clearing forests for thousands of years. Europe has lost 50 percent to 70 percent of its original forest, much of it during the Middle Ages. China has lost 50 percent of its forest since 1700, and the United States has lost 30 percent since Europeans arrived.

Estimates for the total amount of forest lost in the world since the dawn of agriculture, some 8,000 years ago, range from 20 percent to 50 percent.

A dramatic illustration of the connection between population and deforestation occurred in the middle of the 14th century when

Rainforests are in danger as growing populations encroach.

the Black Death wiped out one-third of Europe's population. With fewer people, large deforested areas grew back again. As the population rebounded in the 1500s and 1600s, and human activities increased, large areas of forest were again cut down.

Is forest destruction accelerating? No, and yes.

The temperate zone forests of Russia, North America, and Europe have actually expanded somewhat over the past 40 years. But the situation is the opposite for the world's tropical forests where surrounding populations are growing rapidly. In Central America, 50 percent to 70 percent may have been lost, while in Brazil—which has one-third of the world's tropical forest—about 14 percent of the forest has been cut down just since 1978.

Why do people cut down the rainforest? In Latin America, cattle ranching is the single largest cause of forest destruction. In parts of Asia, much of the forest is cut for simple firewood. In western India, the rainforest is gradually being hacked away to make room for new mango orchards, peanut fields, and lime quarries.

Because rainforests have such abundant plant growth, you might think that the land would be good for farming. But the jungle trees that grow there have different needs than crops. The soils often turn out to be thin and—once the tree canopy is removed—sun-baked. Farming fails, leaving the land barren and useless, providing neither functioning ecosystem nor productive farmland.

In Brazil, the fastest rate of destruction occurred in the 1980s, when an area the size of the state of Massachusetts was destroyed every year. By 1998, all of Sweden, plus some, could fit into the deforested Amazon. In the early 1990s, rich countries boldly pledged $1.5 billion for a World Bank project to protect Brazilian rainforests. So there is hope for the remaining forest.

However, as long as population continues to grow—and rainforest countries have some of the fastest population growth rates in the world—there will be continued pressure to cut down forests. If the population in the region goes up, and those people desperately need land, or food, or wood, or animals, and the rainforest is their only chance, will they exercise restraint for some long-term good? Would you?

SPECIES EXTINCTION

The extinction problem presents us with a simple equation: more people equal fewer wild animals. As human population has surged, the populations of numerous other species have fallen, many to the point of extinction. Humans cause extinction by destroying or altering habitats, overhunting, polluting, and introducing foreign species.

Species extinction differs from all the other problems we've discussed in that it is irreversible. Theoretically, everything else could be corrected—given enough time and effort. Tropical forests can be replanted, topsoil can be replenished; even aquifers will, in thousands of years, fill up again. However, when a species is gone, it's gone for good.

> "The one process now going on that will take millions of years to correct is the loss of genetic and species diversity by the destruction of natural habitats. This is the folly our descendents are least likely to forgive us."
>
> Edward O. Wilson, *A Primer of Population Biology*, 1971.
> Harvard University biologist

Through most of the history of the world, extinction has occurred at a very slow rate (the mass eradication of the dinosaurs some 65 million years ago was one of several significant exceptions). Scientists call this natural extinction the *background rate*. Estimates of the background rate range from about two species every ten years, to twenty or thirty in one year.

Beginning about thirty years ago, concern began to develop that extinction loomed for certain animals such as the whale, rhinoceros, mountain gorilla, condor, whooping crane, and tiger. As a result, the practice of identifying such animals as "endangered" began. Efforts were made to preserve their habitats, to stop hunting them, and to cease putting harmful chemicals in their environments. Some of these animals have been saved from imminent extinction, although for most the prospects for long-term survival are not good.

By and large, the extinctions that you hear about today do not involve well-known species. Most are plants, insects, birds, and microorganisms from the tropical rainforests. And strange as it sounds, many of these living things have never even been identified by science.

In the last decade, ecologists and biologists have been sounding the alarm about the extinction of *thousands* of anonymous species. We now hear incredible numbers—twenty-thousand, thirty thousand, even fifty thousand species passing into extinction *every* year.

These are what scientists call "inferred extinctions." This is how it works. In recent years, scientists studying the rainforests

LOSS OF BIODIVERSITY

Extinctions are part of a larger ecological problem that biologists call the loss of *biodiversity*. Biodiversity means the variety of organisms found within a geological area. When humans build a shopping mall on top of a wetlands —a living community of plants and animals—the biodiversity of the area is diminished. One species (our own) has been substituted for hundreds, or thousands, of others.

Loss of biodiversity also has happened in agriculture as farmers have favored high-yield strains of wheat, corn, or other crops. In the past, a wheat field or a corn field might have a variety of plant strains. Not all would give high yields perhaps, but they had different resistances to disease, droughts, and pests. With today's monoculture— agriculture based on a single plant variety or strain—an entire crop is vulnerable to a single blight or infestation. The Irish Potato Famine of the 1840s was the result of a monoculture. When the blight killed the potato plants, there were no other crops to fall back on. Since 1900, about three-quarters of the genetic diversity of agricultural crops have disappeared. Tree farming, in which forests are replaced with plantations of one or two species of fast-growing tree, is similarly vulnerable to disease, drought, and other natural stresses. Tree plantations don't support as many species of other plants and animals as did the mixed, natural forest.

began to discover insects and plants that were unknown anywhere else. These weren't unique just to the rainforest; they were also unique to a particular section of the rainforest. In 1978, for example, botanist Alwyn Gentry was exploring a ridge in a cloud-forest zone of western Ecuador. He found thirty-eight new plant species, including several with mysteriously black leaves. Before Gentry could get back, the ridge had been completely deforested, the native plants replaced by cacao and other crops.

Based on the frequency with which uncatalogued species were found, and on the rate of rainforest destruction, scientists could estimate or *infer* what species would be lost in a year, even though they couldn't say, in most cases, what species they were. This is the source of reports that we are losing perhaps thirty thousand

THE EMPTY FOREST

A new threat to animals has developed in the rainforest countries; biologists call it "defaunation," or "the empty forest." From Laos to Congo, Brazil to Madagascar, impoverished people desperate to put food in the pot are killing whatever moves. Now, hunters of "bushmeat" have scoured vast areas of tropical forest nearly clean. For the first time, there are large areas of available habitat with few birds or mammals to live in them.

species of animals and plants a year (out of a total of perhaps ten million). One scientist estimated that by the year 2040, between seventeen and thirty-five percent of tropical forest species will be extinct or doomed to extinction.

So far, however, the claim of inferred extinctions remains unproven. Scientists who dispute these numbers—and minimize the problem of extinction in general—point out that the number of documented extinctions since the year 1600 is only 1,033 (although almost everyone agrees that this number is far too low). Others question the value of unidentified beetles, ants, flies, worms, fungi, algae, and viruses.

Scientists alarmed about extinction argue that such creatures could later prove valuable to science or medicine, or that they might play an important role in essential ecosystems.

The debate continues.

SPECIES INVASION

Species invasion is another population-driven environmental problem of which people are only just becoming aware. It may seem incongruous to go from the topic of species extinction to that of species invasion. They sound like opposite problems.

As we will see, often both happen simultaneously. Perhaps instead of species invasion, we should call it species dislocation.

Very simply, it refers to those situations in which people bring some plant or animal, or even a microscopic organism from its native environment to a new one. The new species then causes harm or havoc in the ecosystem.

Plants and animals have been hitching rides with humans for hundreds of years; countless species crossed the oceans when the New World was discovered. The pace has increased dramatically as human populations have grown and as faster modes of transportation have been developed. Not all the exchanges have been bad. For example, many new fruit and vegetable plants were imported from the New World to Europe, improving the diets of the Europeans.

Many, however, have been detrimental—gypsy moths, Dutch elm disease, and sea lamprey, to name just a few. Modern shipping and air transport allows billions of bugs and other animals, viruses, plants, and fungi to move all over the world. They hitch rides on planes, cars, and ships. They stow away in shipping containers, in ballast water, on raw logs, or in human luggage.

Once in their new terrain, these alien species can become a threat. Unchecked by their own natural predators, the invaders may overwhelm weakened native species. They alter vegetation, they compete with or prey on native species, and they sometimes bring new diseases that kill trees or human beings.

The Kudzu vine was imported to the United States from Japan as a decorative vine and has smothered millions of acres in the southern United States. A common home aquarium plant, *Caulerpa taxifolia*, was released into the Mediterranean Sea and now is choking out the native plants. The Nile perch, a big predatory fish introduced into Africa's Lake Victoria in 1962 because it promised good eating, seems to have exterminated at least eighty species of smaller cichlid fishes native to the lakes.

In Hawaii, at least half of all plant species are now exotics. In Florida, which has 40 percent exotics, the Australian Melaleuca tree is covering the Everglades at the rate of 50 acres a day. The Asian Long-horned Beetle, brought over in raw logs, now threatens all U.S. hardwood trees.

Cornell University biologist David Pimentel reports that fifty thousand non-native species have entered U.S. ecosystems in modern times.

A TROUBLED ATMOSPHERE

Over the past one hundred years, the temperature at the Earth's surface has gone up about 1 degree. Today most scientists agree that at least part of that warming is due to emissions of greenhouse gases such as carbon dioxide. The fifteen warmest years on record have all occurred since 1979.

The buildup of greenhouse gases began with the industrial revolution and parallels the buildup of world population. Over the last 150 years, the burning of coal, oil, and natural gas has released some 270 billion tons of carbon into the air in the form of heat-trapping carbon dioxide. As a result, overall atmospheric concentrations of carbon dioxide are about 30 percent higher now than at the start of the industrial revolution.

Over the last twenty-five years—a period in which the world added an unprecedented two billion people—the rate of surface warming has accelerated, amounting to the equivalent of about 3.5 degrees a century. By comparison, the temperature at the depths of the last ice age, 18,000 to 20,000 years ago, was only 5 to 9 degrees cooler than it is today. So, 3.5 degrees would be a big change.

In the last few years, the debate over *global warming* has shifted from the question of whether it was happening at all to whether it is a natural event or one caused by humans. Some scientists believe that natural factors, such as recurring oscillations in ocean surface temperature, may play a role in the last century's warming.

Scientists believe that the degree of global warming we've experienced so far has contributed to heavier and more violent storms (due to increased water vapor in the atmosphere), more severe droughts, and heat waves. Spring is coming about a week earlier in the temperate zones. Icecaps on mountaintops are receding.

are two effects of global warming.

What would happen if the worst-case scenario comes to pass, and the temperature goes up by 3.5 degrees Fahrenheit by 2100? This much warming, the experts say, would bring rising seas, more severe droughts and storms, heat waves and floods, along with broad shifts in climatic and agricultural zones that would benefit some regions but seriously harm others. In one of the worst case scenarios, the 2-mile thick Antarctic ice shelves could melt, a catastrophic event that would raise the level of the ocean 17 feet, flooding coastal areas almost everywhere.

So far, attempts to get the advanced countries to reduce their carbon dioxide emissions have had disappointing results. Meanwhile, as the poorer countries develop, they contribute a bigger share of carbon dioxide emissions.

COASTS AND CORAL REEFS

More than half of humanity—some 3.2 billion people, according to some estimates—live and work within 120 miles of a seacoast. Two-thirds live within 250 miles of a coast. All this human activity has taken its toll: half the world's coastal wetlands, including salt marshes, have disappeared. Millions of hectares of mangrove forests—multi-rooted trees on the edge of the sea—have been destroyed or grossly degraded. And close to 70 percent of the world's beaches are eroding at rapid rates because of human impacts.

The most tragic damage of all is to coral reefs. They are the rainforests of the sea, supporting perhaps one million species. They are overfished, dynamited, poisoned by sewage, pummeled by ships' anchors, broken by recreational divers, and bleached by unseasonably warm temperatures. Corals are particularly susceptible to global warming because they live at the upper end of their temperature tolerance. As a result, a rise of just 2 degrees Centigrade can be disastrous. Global warming has already killed most of the coral in the Indian Ocean and in areas of the western and eastern Pacific. A report by the environmental group, Greenpeace, says global warming will destroy all the world's coral reefs in the

Coral reefs are in grave danger of being lost forever.

next thirty years unless predicted levels of climate change are avoided. The Great Barrier Reef, which is 1,200 kilometers long and about 500 meters wide, is the largest reef system in the world and the biggest structure made by living organisms. Most of the coral is two million years old, although the oldest parts date back eighteen million years.

CHAPTER SEVEN
Living in an Overcrowded World

We've already seen that too many people can drain the world's natural resources and disrupt its ecosystems. As we learned, however, sometimes the negative effects from such actions can take a long time to trickle down. Societies can even enjoy a period of false prosperity while they "overshoot" their carrying capacity. This means that many of the repercussions of overpopulation may not have been felt yet. Even global warming is apparently still in its early stages.

This is not to say that overpopulation does not cause plenty of problems in the here and now. Common sense tells us that a society that is doubling its population every twenty-five or thirty years will be hard pressed to provide the necessary education, jobs, health care, or sanitary services that are necessary for a good quality of life. All those additional people often end up living in extreme poverty in vast slums or shantytowns such as those in and around Bombay, Mexico City, or Calcutta.

These places are ideal breeding grounds for disease. Shantytowns often have no toilets or clean water, and their residents are crowded into damp dirty rooms, often sleeping six, seven, or more to a room. People living in these conditions are often malnourished and suffer from diarrhea or pneumonia, two leading causes of child and infant mortality in poor countries. Epidemics of cholera and typhus are commonplace in these areas.

These are a few of the countless examples of physical and social ills that are found in conjunction with large, rapidly growing populations. Yet, the complex interplay between all these factors sometimes makes it impossible to say with absolute certainty that overpopulation is the *cause* of these problems. For example, some have argued that *poverty* is the cause of these poor living conditions and that poverty is the result of things not necessarily linked to overpopulation, such as social injustice, corrupt political systems, and economic inequalities.

POLLUTION AND POPULATION

Most, if not all, pollution problems are made worse by overpopulation. Certain pollution problems, for example, don't even arise until large numbers of people become involved. A few people discharging human waste into a river may cause no long-term effects. But when a thousand people or a hundred thousand start doing it, the river's ability to cleanse itself is overwhelmed and it becomes polluted. The same is true of automobile pollution. The exhaust from a few thousand cars may be dispersed by the winds, but a few hundred thousand cars can easily overwhelm the dispersal capacity of the atmosphere, resulting in life-threatening smog.

The air may be somewhat cleaner in North America, after a twenty-year antipollution effort and billions of dollars spent on scrubbers, catalytic converters, and other technology, but in Eastern Europe, Russia, China, India, and other countries, pollution is still a serious problem.

China, for example, has some of the dirtiest rivers in the world. Although China enacted strict antipollution laws in the 1990s, flagrant violations occur without any serious investigation. This is especially true in the rural areas, where local factories often ignore antipollution laws. China is expanding its efforts to combat water pollution, but even if it can get its rivers cleaned up in a few decades, the prospects for its air are poor. China has huge coal deposits and plans to burn this heavily polluting fuel in all its future power plants.

A GROWING MEDIUM FOR DISEASE

Despite medical advances that have wiped out many diseases, many scientists believe that the world today is particularly vulnerable to new epidemics or even a pandemic. Infectious diseases, as we saw, thrive in dense concentrations of people. Humans are the "medium" in which infectious diseases grow and flourish.

Hence, the more gigantic the population, the more favorable the conditions for the spread of disease, especially among the several billion living in overcrowded and unsanitary conditions in poor villages, slums, and sprawling shantytowns where key disease carriers, such as insects and rats, thrive.

Viruses and other microbes have an additional advantage in today's world because of globalization and rapid modes of transportation. We saw, in the case of species invasion, how readily animals like snakes and rats have been able to stow away on ships and even airplanes. It is even easier for microscopic viruses and microbes to cross oceans and jump from continent to continent.

In earlier times, when long-distance travel was by ship, people who were carrying diseases would show symptoms in the course of a voyage, and measures could be taken to quarantine the sick when the ship came to port. In the age of jet travel, however, a person unknowingly incubating a disease can board a plane, travel 12,000 miles, pass through customs and immigration, take a domestic carrier to a remote destination, and still not develop symptoms for several days. Along the way, this person could infect many other people.

Prior to the outbreak of AIDS in the early 1980s, public health workers were beginning to believe that perhaps infectious diseases were a thing of the past, that they had been completely conquered by antibiotics, vaccines, and other medical advances. Since then, however, a host of infectious diseases have been identified as a threat.

Starting in 1995, a new strain of cholera began surfacing in Africa and Asia, killing thousands of people. There have been outbreaks of diphtheria in Laos, Thailand, and the United States;

dengue and the more serious dengue hemorrhagic fever in India, Malaysia, and Venezuela; various forms of meningitis in parts of Europe, North America, and West Africa; and Ebola in sub-Saharan Africa. West Nile Fever, a disease native to the Middle East, began showing up in the northeastern United States in 1999. It spreads by mosquitoes, which prey on both birds and humans.

RAINFOREST DESTRUCTION

Another factor contributing to disease is the destruction of the rainforest. Because the rainforests contain at least half of the world's plant and animal species, and because all living things carry viruses, the rainforests are also the world's largest reservoir of viruses. When people invade these previously uninhabited areas, they can become host to previously unknown viruses. Both AIDS and the deadly Ebola virus are thought to have originated in the rainforest. As author Richard Preston writes in *The Hot Zone*, a book that warns of the danger of new epidemics resulting from rainforest destruction, "When viruses come out of an ecosystem, they tend to spread in waves through the human population, like echoes from the dying biosphere."

SPREAD OF AIDS

What made AIDS turn into a worldwide epidemic? The simplest answer is the surge in population. As Africa's population grew, it brought with it social changes and massive environmental upheaval. Truck routes were built into the rural interior. Wars uprooted entire populations from the area where AIDS is believed to have originated. Cities began to spill over into what had been virgin territory, bringing with them new patterns of sexual behavior and prostitution. The disease spread to the rest of the world through American and European intravenous drug use and homosexual bathhouse activity, as well as the contamination of blood supplies and the spread of those blood supplies around the world. Currently, some thirty million people are infected, and there still is no sign of a cure.

AIDS WILL HAVE LITTLE IMPACT ON POPULATION GROWTH

There is a common misconception that AIDS is acting as a brake on population growth. In earlier periods of human history, when the human population was much smaller, an epidemic could have a major impact on population. In the past several hundred years, however, the population has easily rebounded from large epidemics. One reason is that medical science and public health authorities are better able to slow the spread of a disease, even if they can't cure it. The other reason is exponential growth: modern populations are so large that they can easily make up for large numbers of deaths. The influenza pandemic of 1918-1919 took twenty million people, but population continued to skyrocket worldwide. China lost thirty million to starvation between 1958 and 1962, and yet today China is the world's most populous nation, with 1.3 billion people.

MIGRATION

What do people do when they are faced with population-related problems such as crowding, disease, malnutrition, political instability, war, housing shortages, unemployment, pollution, poor sanitation, and environmental degradation? Not surprisingly, many of them pick up and move. They go in search of a better life. They migrate. There are an estimated 100 million migrants in the world today.

The twentieth century witnessed many of history's largest and most dramatic migrations. More than eighteen million people immigrated to the United States between 1900 and 1930, and another eighteen million between 1970 and 1997. The Population

Reference Bureau estimates that 125 million people are living outside their country of birth. In New York City, traditionally a destination for immigrants, the percentage of foreign-born people in the population has soared to as high as 40 percent, according to a 1999 Census Bureau report.

The desperation of some migrants has been underscored in recent years in reports of illegal immigrants—many of them from China—who perish in airtight shipping containers, sweltering trucks, or other cargo carriers. These cases have uncovered networks of criminals—human smugglers—that charge illegal immigrants fees in the tens of thousands of dollars to get them across borders and ultimately to Europe or the United States.

ECO-MIGRATION

Eco-migrants are people forced to uproot themselves because of environmental degradation. The number of people fleeing deforested, desertified, or flooded lands is currently estimated at about twenty-five million and is continuing to rise.

Swelling populations are crowding people into vulnerable or dangerous areas that are prone to floods and mudslides. When storms hit, more people are in harm's way. For example, the Choluteca region of Honduras was hit by Hurrricane Fifi in 1974 and Hurricane Mitch in 1999. Both hurricanes were of similar force, but Hurricane Mitch killed twice as many people. Why? Between the hurricanes, thousands of people had moved onto such dangerous areas as the Choluteca River floodplain and the nearby steep, highly erodible slopes.

Looming over the problem of eco-migration is the question of change. According to some climate models, even moderate warming might reduce Mexico's agricultural output more than a third, putting many people on the move.

Sea-level rise may be the biggest impetus to eco-migration, since more than one billion people and a third of the world's croplands are less than 3 meters above sea level. Oceans have already risen between 10 and 25 centimeters in the past century, as warming waters expanded and coasts subsided because of damming and overpumping of fresh water. In recent years, 6-meter-high storm surges have swept 160 kilometers inland in low-lying Bangladesh. Every centimeter of sea-level rise places additional millions of people at risk.

Wars and genocide create refugees—emergency migrants who are often fleeing for their lives. Central Africa witnessed a series of brutal conflicts in the past four decades that have spawned a torrent of refugees from countries such as Rwanda, Angola, Uganda, Ethiopia, Sudan, Somalia, Tanzania, and Zimbabwe. In the 1990s, estimates of the number of refugees in the world ranged from thirteen million to fifteen million.

Famine is another cause of migration. In North Korea, where about two million people have starved from 1995 to 2000 in what United Nations experts call a "slow motion famine," some one hundred thousand or more migrants have sneaked across the Chinese border in search of food or permanent sanctuary.

URBANIZATION

People moving from the country to the city—urbanization—is one of the most dramatic demographic changes of the twentieth century. Demographer Philip M. Hauser of the University of Chicago called it the "population implosion."

In less than two centuries (1800 to 1990), the fraction of people who lived in cities surged from perhaps one in fifty to nearly one in two. In 1800, only one city—London—had a million people. Today, 326 cities have at least that many.

As fast as population has been growing, the world's cities are growing even faster. What is causing this change?

In the early stages of industrialization, urbanization took place largely in response to the pull of employment opportunities in cities. Factory and office jobs were more numerous and paid better than farming. More recently, however, the movement from countryside to city has been more the result of rural push than of urban pull. This push is a result of a strange side effect of population pressures. In many Third World countries, farming land has been gradually divided into even smaller plots. How has this happened? When a farmer passes on his farm to his children, he divides it up between them, or at least between the sons. They, in turn, grow old and divide the land between their heirs. So, with each succeeding generation, the land has grown smaller and smaller, until the plots become so small that people can no longer make a living from them.

In more affluent countries, such as the United States, farmers are throwing in the towel because they can't compete with agribusiness—giant corporations that farm on a huge mechanized

SHANTYTOWNS

They are called *ranchos* in Venezuela, *favelas* in Brazil, and *colonias* in Mexico. All are shantytowns, sprawling squatter settlements that surround cities in Latin America, Asia, and Africa. Between 40 and 50 percent of the people in the Southern Hemisphere live in these settlements—roughly one billion people.

They are home to poor families that come from the countryside seeking opportunity in the big city but don't have enough money to buy or rent a place to live. Instead, they build their own homes out of discarded materials, such as scrap lumber, plastic, cardboard, rubber tires, and sheet metal. Shantytowns have no plumbing or sewers. Sometimes a single water spigot must serve thousands of people.

A favela in Brazil.

Shantytowns are often plagued by violent crime, and, with little law enforcement, some have become havens for drug lords. Because of crowding and flimsy construction, residents of shantytowns are more vulnerable to natural disasters, such as floods or mudslides. In December of 1999, a deluge in Caracas, Venezuela, washed thousands of the rickety structures down the 6,000-foot slopes around the city, killing as many as 30,000 people, and leaving 150,000 homeless.

The five hundred or so *favelas* that encircle Rio de Janeiro have become so notorious that tourist groups from all nations come in jeep convoys to see the jumble of cinder-block, tin-roofed homes. Guides call these trips "reality tours."

scale. As a result, many rural towns in America are becoming depopulated, as people move to cities in search of jobs.

In the United States, sprawling cities are meeting at the edges, forming huge urban corridors, or megalopolises, as in the Washington to Boston corridor. In some of the developing countries, the rapid rate of migration to cities has caused the urban population to outstrip the availability of basic services, such as water, sewerage, transportation, and electricity.

Even the large cities of poorer countries, such as Rio de Janeiro or São Paulo, Brazil, are surrounded by crowded shantytowns in which the houses are usually no more than a few pieces of wood or cardboard.

Urbanization has one positive effect on population growth. People living in cities tend to have fewer children than people in rural areas. So, as more people move to cities, population growth may slow in the developing countries.

CHAPTER EIGHT
Fear of Shrinking

In May of 2000, the Bandai Corporation, a major Japanese toy maker, announced that it would pay employees 1 million yen, or $10,000, for every baby they would have after the second child. Japanese couples have an average of only 1.38 children, and the government and major businesses have been encouraging them to have more.

Rewards for more children? Isn't a lower birth rate a good thing?

In fact, Japan isn't the only country trying to raise its birth rate. The United Nations reports that twenty-three nations—most of them in Europe—are making a similar effort. All have fertility rates below the replacement rate of 2.1 babies per woman. In the United Kingdom, the rate is just 1.7, in Italy it is down to 1.2, and in Spain it is just 1.15 (dropping below 1 in some parts of Spain). In the United States, fertility is just a shade under replacement at two babies per woman.

BIRTH DEARTH

Are these nations right to worry about a "birth dearth"?

Demographers in these countries now churn out the same kind of projections that were once used to show the effects of runaway growth but that are now used to show the dire effects of shrink-age. If Japan continues on its present path, they say, population will dwindle to five hundred by the end of the millennium and to a *single person* in A.D. 3500!

Of course, no one expects this to happen, anymore than anyone expects the Earth to become an expanding ball of human bodies. But how can there be too many people and at the same time not enough people?

The Earth's population is divided into two demographic worlds. Although population is holding or going down in most of the more developed countries, it is rapidly expanding in the less developed countries—where most of the people live. Think of it this way: 20 percent of the world may be shrinking, but 80 percent of it is growing. Of course, that's still better than having 100 percent of the world growing. So, why do these developed nations fear shrinkage so much?

STRENGTH IN NUMBERS

Societies have long considered a large population to be a sign of strength and vitality. In the past, more populous countries had bigger armies and were more secure from attack. The ancient Romans, for example, were encouraged to multiply so that there would be more people who could settle, guard, and administer all the lands of the empire.

The idea that there is strength in numbers persists today. It is particularly strong in situations where hostile ethnic groups live in uneasy proximity to each other, such as Hindus and Muslims in India and Pakistan, Hutus and Tutsis in Africa, or Palestinians and Jews in Israel. Often one group will try to *out-reproduce* the other so as to have a stronger presence. In the densely populated Gaza Strip, for example, women—mostly Palestinians—have an average of 7.3 children, making it the fastest growing country in the world.

Some of the anxiety in the shrinking nations over declining

fertility probably stems from a similar fear of being vastly out-numbered by people of other cultures and races. Japan, for example, lived for millennia in the shadow of its neighbor China and only gained autonomy through economic strength. Now, Japan is shrinking as China keeps growing—and developing.

In 1950, two-thirds of the world's population lived in developing countries; by 2050, it will be nine-tenths. The journalist Ben Wattenberg in his 1987 book, *The Birth Dearth*, expressed alarm that falling birth rates in the Western democracies would result in a world in which the values of democracy and Western civilization would lose influence. He also argued that the balance of power could shift as well and that America needed more young people in order to maintain a strong army.

GROWTH EQUALS PROSPERITY

Countries also worry about population shrinkage because they fear it will result in economic decline. Although growing populations in poor countries often increase poverty, growing populations in developed countries can stimulate the economy. Think of it this way: If you have a product or a service to sell, and every year there are more people to sell it to, that's going to be good for business. A steadily increasing demand for products and services usually means an expanding economy.

Some economists, such as Julian Simon, took this idea a step further and challenged the whole notion of too many people. Far from being a social ill and a threat to the planet, he said, population growth should be thought of as a *good thing*: as population has increased, so has the quality of life. The majority of people in the world, Simon argued, are better off than previous generations. They're healthier, wealthier, and live longer. The bad consequences of population growth—shantytowns, shortages, poverty, and the like—are only temporary, he maintained, because society eventually solves these problems, and the overall quality of life continues to rise.

FEAR OF GRAYING

A more immediate concern of shrinking countries, however, is their aging populations. When a country begins to have fewer babies, the younger generation is smaller than the older ones, and the average age of the population goes up. In Japan, for example, the median age is expected to increase from 41 to 49 by 2050.

Demographers use graphs called population pyramids to illustrate the different age profiles of populations.

The pyramids of the developing countries, for example, have a very broad base and a narrow top reflecting the large number of young people in their populations. But the populations of the more developed countries have a bulge in the middle because of the larger proportion of people in middle age. In the United States, that bulge corresponds to the baby boomers, the large generation born between 1945 and 1965.

Demographers call this a *graying population* because the proportion of older people is growing. Graying populations face special economic challenges because they have fewer workers than retired people. Retired people collect benefits from such systems as Social Security and Medicare that depend on taxes paid by the current working population. Hence, the thinking goes, if there are too many people collecting benefits and fewer workers contributing to the pool of money, the system could go bankrupt.

Population Pyramids

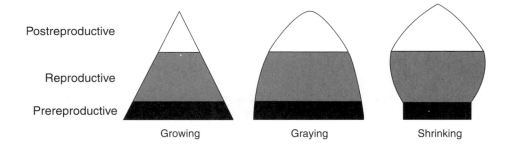

Postreproductive

Reproductive

Prereproductive

Growing   Graying   Shrinking

Immigration is one way for a country to offset a shrinking birth rate. Europe and Japan mostly shun immigration, but the United States, with a birth rate of only two children per woman, has continued to grow because it accepts more legal immigrants annually than all the other nations of the world combined. The Census Bureau projects that the U.S. population will increase from its present 284 million to nearly 400 million by 2050, with the increase due almost entirely to immigrants and their offspring.

REBUTTALS

Many analysts dispute the various problems attributed to population shrinkage.

Demographer John Bongaarts of the Population Council says that "birth dearth" figures for the Western countries are misleading. Women in these countries are still having about two children, he says, but they're having them later in life, a trend that the census takers haven't taken into account. Hence, the birth rates for these countries may start to rise as women in their thirties or even forties—who were assumed to have finished having children—add another child, or have a long-delayed first child.

Others argue that the problems of a graying population will not be as grave as people imagine. For example, an older population may mean a smaller proportion of workers, but it also means fewer children, a group that requires expensive day care and schooling. Some analysts feel that the strain of supporting more elderly will be offset by the decreased need to support so many children. Later retirement ages may also help to offset the burden on younger workers of supporting systems such as Social Security.

In response to worries about loss of military strength, others argue that a technologically advanced military doesn't depend on soldiers as did armies of the past. If strength were in simple numbers, then China and India would be the most powerful countries in the world, and the United States would be a distant third.

Finally, advocates of population control state that alarm over shrinkage and graying populations, and attempts to fix it by increasing immigration or trying to raise birth rates, only postpone the problem. The population can't grow indefinitely, they point out. Sooner or later, they say, the problems of shrinking will have to be faced. Waiting will only make things worse.

CHAPTER NINE

Population Control

The population explosion didn't happen because women suddenly started having more babies. It happened because fewer of those babies died and women continued having the same number. Hence, it might be said that the success of "death control" (public health improvements) had caused the problem, and its solution, most people recognized, would have to come from "*birth control*" (contraception).

In the 1960s, international efforts got under way to bring birth control to the developing world. In the 1970s, the two most populous countries, India and China, started their own programs. Unlike the international programs, which were entirely voluntary, the programs in India and China involved laws and coercion.

Almost immediately population growth began to slow. Childbearing decreased worldwide, from a global average of 5 children per woman in 1950 to 2.7 today.

BIRTH CONTROL METHODS

People use a variety of contraceptive methods today. Both men and women can be surgically sterilized, which makes pregnancy impossible. Women can take medication in the form of pills or small implants under the skin; they can have intrauterine devices

ANCIENT MEANS OF BIRTH CONTROL

Birth control may involve modern medical technology today, but the people of the past had their own methods:

■ **PROLONGED BREASTFEEDING:** Women who are breastfeeding generally don't ovulate and hence can't become pregnant. Hunter-gatherer women would prolong the breastfeeding period beyond the normal period of one year for an additional year or two to space out their children.

■ **INDUCING ABORTION:** In ancient Rome, women tried to induce abortion by riding a cart along a bumpy road. They also used a potion made from Pennyroyal, a member of the mint family, which has long been used for that purpose.

■ **INFANTICIDE:** In many ancient cultures, including Greece and Rome, it was an accepted practice to expose unwanted children in the wild, where they died of cold, starvation, or attack by predators. Weak or deformed infants were frequent victims of this practice, but others were left to die because of illegitimacy, poverty, or because they were girls and perceived as more of a financial liability than boys. A fortunate few were rescued by childless women who raised them as their own. Others were gathered up by cruel opportunists who raised the children as slaves or prostitutes. Infanticide wasn't curbed in the Roman Empire until late in the fourth century, at the dawn of the Christian era.

■ **BARRIER CONTRACEPTIVES:** Condoms were originally made from animal intestines. Ancient people also fashioned primitive diaphragms out of cloth, leaves, cotton fibers, and, in the case of the ancient Egyptians, crocodile dung.

■ **ORAL CONTRACEPTIVES:** Scientists believe that the ancient Greeks and Romans even had oral contraceptives. The sap of a now-extinct plant called silphion (a species of giant fennel), was supposed to prevent pregnancy. The seeds of Queen Anne's lace, a distant relative of silphion, are used as a contraceptive in India and in the Appalachian Mountains of the United States today.

(IUDs) inserted, or they can use contraceptive aids such as diaphragms, sponges, or foams before having sex. Men can use condoms, which have the added benefit of offering protection against AIDS and other sexually transmitted diseases. Each method has advantages and disadvantages.

The final method of birth control is abortion, or ending a pregnancy by surgery or medication before the fetus is fully developed. Abortion is legal in some countries, illegal in others. In some countries, abortion has been used as a standard method of birth control. In many countries, even where it is legal, as in the United States, abortion is a highly controversial issue. Many people have strong religious or ethical objections to it.

GETTING TO THE BOTTOM OF GROWTH

Birth control efforts had succeeded. In the 1950s, less than 10 percent of the people in the developing world were using contraceptives; today, about half do. Even so, science still wasn't sure what factors caused people to have smaller families. There had been so many different approaches—education, persuasion, improved availability of contraceptives, and incentives—that no one was quite sure which methods were best. What worked in one country didn't work in another. It was a subtle and complicated issue.

Without understanding why childbearing slowed, demographers can't say whether or not the trend will continue, nor can they help it along in places where fertility is still high. So there is still a lot of disagreement and controversy over population control. Some of the world's success can be attributed to China's radical "one-child" policy, which many have condemned as a human rights abuse. Meanwhile, many people continue to believe that population shouldn't be controlled at all.

CHINA: SUCCESS AT A STEEP PRICE

Under Chairman Mao Zedong, China's communist ruler from 1949 until his death in 1976, China's citizens were encouraged to have as many children as possible. By the late 1970s, however, the country was staggering under a population that was fast approaching one billion. Its new leaders decided that China should not have more than 650 to 750 million people and decreed that couples should have only two children. Couples who obeyed the ruling got better housing and other benefits. The program succeeded in bringing down the average number of children per woman from six to about two.

In 1979, however, a census showed that the population had already reached the one billion mark. The government, a dictatorship, then took the drastic measure of demanding that new families have only one child. Some eighty thousand officials were dispersed around the country to enforce the campaign. Licenses were required to have a baby. People were fired from jobs and fined for having more than one child.

Strong-arm tactics were common. Horror stories emerged about women forced to have abortions, some of them late-term (even when the baby was almost ready to be born). There were also reports of parents aborting or even killing girl babies because they wanted their one child to be a boy. (Male children are traditionally more valued in Chinese families because they carry on the family name.)

Today, China still defends the one-child program, though not the excesses it created. Population stands at 1.3 billion; without the program, they say, it would be 1.6 billion. Some rules have been relaxed, especially for farmers, who need children to help with the work. Laws requiring baby permits have been eliminated in many places, and the practice of forcing women to undergo abortions and sterilization has been curtailed.

INDIA—THE REWARD SYSTEM

India has about a billion people. By 2050 it is expected to have 1.5 billion—more than any other country, including China. As in most places, the poor people are the fastest growing group.

Because of a history of famines and epidemics, India has long recognized the need for population control. In the 1970s, a coercive, punitive program of sterilization caused a temporary backlash against all birth control efforts.

CHINA'S LITTLE EMPERORS

Only-children are supposed to be spoiled. So what happens in a country such as China, where a one-child policy has been in effect since 1979?

Answer: A generation of "Little Emperors." Since 1983, more than 320 million babies have been born in China, the vast majority of them only-children. From birth, they are indulged and pampered by parents and grandparents. Those from affluent families are dressed in fancy outfits, showered with toys, and given every kind of enrichment lesson.

All the material goods that typically would have been spread among two or more children are lavished on the "onlies." And since grandparents have fewer grandchildren, they don't mind spoiling the ones they have. Some people find it shocking, in a communist country, to see parents spending more of their income on one child than earlier generations had spent on eight.

A grandmother with a grandchild in China

Now, a new approach—using rewards instead of punishments—is achieving dramatic results in one of India's states—Andhra Pradesh. The goal is to convince couples to be sterilized after one or two children. Those who do receive government benefits. For poor people this can mean a cash award, a house, a plot of land, a well, or a loan. There are even bonus prizes such as wall clocks and steel pots, and trips to the state capital.

The state's chief minister, Chandrababu Naidu, flies by a helicopter from one village to another, selling his ideas at mass meetings. Those with big families are publicly scolded, and the crowd is enlisted to condemn or cheer, just like on an American daytime talk show.

A *New York Times* report tells how Naidu told one resistant farmer, a father of four who wanted to have more children, that the state would give him a house if he had the operation. "I will definitely have it done," the farmer quickly promised.

The program has dramatically increased the number of sterilizations in the state over the past five years. The fertility rate is now close to the stabilization rate of 2.1 children per woman. That is in sharp contrast to other large states, where women are having an average of four children each.

For all its success, the program conflicts with today's more popular philosophy—adopted at the United Nations 1994 conference on population—that better education and improved social status for women is the best way to reduce birthrates. That approach seems to have worked elsewhere in India—in the much smaller province of Kerala, which achieved lower birthrates in the late 1980s.

Kerala is often cited as a model of what high rates of female literacy and good health care can accomplish in lowering fertility. The situation is much different in Andhra Pradesh, where half the women are still illiterate and are married by age 15.

The clashing approaches to controlling population mirror a larger debate in India and elsewhere in Asia. Is social progress for women the best way to reduce the number of children they will bear? Or should governments aggressively seek to reduce fertility with incentives and persuasion before the social progress is achieved?

The fact that both programs have been successful underscores a familiar lesson in population control. Different things work in different places at different times, and no one approach is a universal answer.

A MILLION MISSING GIRLS

Females are hardier than males, and, as a result, there are usually more of them in any population. In the United States, Europe, and Japan—places where male and female babies are treated equally—there are about 105 females for every 100 males.

But a different picture emerges in much of Asia, North Africa, and parts of Latin America—places where there are cultural biases in favor of boy babies. In recent years, censuses began to show that there were more males than females. In all of South Asia, for example, there are only 94 females for every 100 males. In India, a 1991 census found only 93 females for every 100 males. And in China the 1990 census found just 93.8 females for every 100 males.

What was going on? If the normal proportions were 105 women for every 100 men, but instead there were only 94 women, that meant there were an average of nine women "missing" out of every hundred. The Indian economist Amartya Sen gathered figures from around the world and calculated that an incredible one hundred million females were missing from all around the world. He concluded that these women had disappeared as infants through a mixture of abortions, infanticide, and deliberate undernourishment leading to death from neglect.

"If a boy gets sick, the parents may send him to the hospital at once," a Chinese official told the *New York Times*. "But, if a girls gets sick, the parents may say to themselves, "Well, we'll see how she is tomorrow."

This problem was particularly acute in China during the one-child policy era because so many parents wanted the only child to be a son. Medical tests taken during pregnancy can tell whether a couple will have a boy or a girl, and it is believed that many women aborted girl babies. A total of thirty million females were judged missing in China alone.

INTERNATIONAL POPULATION CONFERENCES

About once every ten years, the United Nations sponsors an international conference on population. Representatives of nations and various organizations come together to discuss the problem and to pledge money to various programs. Often these conferences signal dramatic shifts in thinking about population control.

At the 1974 conference in Bucharest, for example, the poorer countries attacked *family planning* programs as attempts by richer nations to keep their numbers down. There were charges of "racism" (the poorer countries are mostly nonwhite, the developed countries mostly white) and of "neocolonialism" (the poorer countries were former colonies of the European countries and had been exploited by them). Instead of birth control, the poor countries demanded help with their economic development, giving rise to the slogan "development is the best contraceptive." Behind it was the belief that once the countries were developed, their birth rates would naturally fall, following the pattern in the richer countries.

At the 1984 conference in Mexico City, the United States showed how attitudes about birth control had changed under President Ronald Reagan. The American delegates shocked the other countries by announcing that the United States no longer believed that population growth had a negative impact on a country's economic progress. The United States withdrew its support from many programs and stopped being a major force for population control for the next eight years.

At the 1994 conference in Cairo, the one that set the tone for today's policy stance, many delegates complained that population thinking had become too negative, that environmentalists used cold phrases such as "cost per avoided child," and described human population growth as "a cancer on the Earth."

At Cairo, the focus was on positive population thinking, with emphasis on the rights and reproductive health of women. This approach is based on evidence that the more education women have, the more likely they are to have small families. In many countries today, girls receive little schooling, are expected to marry early and raise many children, and have no independent lives outside of their homes. However, girls who remain in school tend to marry later and have smaller families. More education also gives women more opportunities to work outside of the home and to have, in a career, sources of fulfillment and self-esteem other than having children.

After fifty years of experimentation and theorizing, the world still has no surefire way of reducing population in a free society. Some say the simplest, most direct approach may still be the answer. They point to studies showing that ready access to birth control is the most effective way of reducing births. Mimicking a previous slogan, three American researchers—Bryan Robey, Shea O. Rutstein, and Leo Morris—came up with a new variant, "contraception is the best contraceptive," in their article, "The Family Decline in Developing Countries."

Just because there is a certain amount of built-in growth to the population doesn't mean the world can't offset the momentum. The current population momentum might be slowed in part by changing the behavior of adolescents, especially those in the less developed world, advises Dr. John Bongaarts of the Population Council. Women in the underdeveloped countries often begin having children in their teens. If all these women delayed having children by five years, the rise in world population due to momentum could be reduced by about 1.2 billion over the next century, according to Bongaarts. Ways to raise the age of childbearing include raising the legal age of marriage and prolonging the education of girls, especially in secondary schools. Women who delay having their first child until they are in their early to mid-twenties generally have smaller families.

CHAPTER TEN
Time to Connect the Dots

How do we sum up our situation? The population problem has too many dimensions to yield to one simple summary. As we have seen, overpopulation is not just about numbers of people. It's about people's relationship to the Earth; it's about quality of life and life expectancy; it's about diet, fresh water, big cities, migration, and war.

There's no simple equation, no real answer to a question such as "How many people can the Earth support?" But there are trends, and clear warning signs, and problems that are already here.

Let's start with the numbers. Birth rates are falling. Demographers can actually foresee a time when population will stabilize and maybe even begin to go down. That's the good news. The bad news is that projected stabilization is still about two hundred years away. Think of the population as a freight train running down a hill. The brakes have been put on—somewhat—and there's the sound of steel screeching against steel, but the train will coast for some distance before it actually stops. Freight trains don't stop on a dime, and neither do huge populations. They both have something called momentum.

Population momentum occurs when there's a large proportion of young people in a population. A younger population has more reproducing couples than an older one, so there is more potential for growth. Our world population has the largest generation of young people ever—about 1.05 billion between the ages of 15 and 24. That group, mostly in the developing countries, guarantees that our population will keep on rolling despite the drop in the average number of children. It would keep growing even if the fertility rate immediately dropped to replacement level.

So, screeching brakes and all, our freight train isn't going to visibly slow for some time. Population will continue to grow at the rate of a billion people every twelve or thirteen years for another twenty-five years. That will give us about eight billion people by 2025. The next billion will take about twice as long to reach, giving us a population of around nine billion by 2050. Then things will slow in earnest, with the next billion taking about 150 years and population increase finally coming to a halt sometime after 2200.

Bear in mind that these are only projections based on current trends. Lots of things could happen to change these numbers. Another great stride forward in life expectancy, for example, could skew these numbers way up. A twenty-first century equivalent of the Black Death could do the opposite. We could also decide to push down harder on the brakes. Our engineer doesn't have his foot all the way down on the pedal—far from it. A world that was determined to stop population growth could slow to one child per couple. That's still a lot of new children. A generation of one billion plus parents in which each couple had an average of only one child could still produce five hundred million plus children—hardly a world birth dearth.

But if the U.N. projections hold true, and we are really only midpoint in a one-hundred-year population explosion, what is it going to be like? It would be nice to look back in history to find something to compare this scenario to, but the world has never seen anything like this before. Never have there been so many people, never such a staggering rate of growth, and never so many changes happening to the world itself.

That is the other half of the equation. It's not just that there are six billion people on Earth, or that, in geological time, this has happened in the blink of an eye. It's the impact of those six—

eight—ten billion people on the Earth. It's the fact that our species has risen to such a position of dominance over the planet that we are changing its very climate, raising its oceans, deciding which other species will live and which will die.

This, then, is humanity's dilemma at the beginning of the twenty-first century. On the one hand, we have a swelling population that may already be pressing up against the Earth's carrying capacity. On the other, we see a collection of ecosystems that, as a direct result of population pressures, are breaking down and becoming unpredictable.

Either one by itself poses a formidable challenge for humanity. If, as seems to be our intent, we are going to try to fit as many people as possible onto the Earth at one time, then you would think we would want an Earth in tip-top condition, with all systems working at maximum efficiency: abundant agricultural harvests, oceans teeming with fish, thriving forests, aquifers filled to the brim. Instead, we have a climate that is hotter and stormier, oceans depleted of fish, shrinking forests and growing deserts, and aquifers that are closer to empty than full, with no prospects for a refill.

UNKNOWN CONSEQUENCES

A human population that grows so fast it begins to run out of food or water for itself is a problem that is terrible enough. Even worse is a human population that grows so fast that it does permanent damage to the Earth and makes it less habitable—not just for itself but for future generations as well. The Easter Islanders had no idea they were destroying their own forest for good. It had always been there, and it always grew back. Somehow, however, they crossed a point of no return and found themselves in a diminished world. A world of no more wood for canoes and beams, a world of fewer animals, a world of constant erosion and water shortages—they started a terrible chain reaction, with results that they never foresaw. As a result, they lost everything that was dear to them.

We like to tell ourselves that we are smarter and have more foresight than these islanders of years ago. But are we? The truth

NIGHTMARE IN INDONESIA

For a sense of the nightmarish chain reactions that population pressures can produce, consider the situation in Indonesia.

Indonesia is one of the most biologically diverse nations on Earth. Spread across its archipelago of thousands of islands are vast tropical rainforests, mangrove swamps, and spectacular coral reefs that are home to millions of plants and animals, including 25 percent of the world's fish.

It is also the fourth most populous country in the world. One hundred years ago, about ten million people lived there. Today, there are more than two hundred million. In the 1990s, an economic boom brought rapid modernization and drew tens of millions of rural Indonesians to the cities. Then the economy collapsed, closing factories and office buildings and leaving millions of workers jobless, hungry, and homeless. In an effort to get back on its feet, Indonesia borrowed $43 billion from the International Monetary Fund. To pay that back, it has had to agreed to sell its natural resources.

Its once vast forests are being ripped up both for timber and to make way for plantations and shrimp farms that will help pay off its debts. Tens of thousands of the urban unemployed fled back to the countryside to work for illegal logging operations or gold mining operations. Others are dealing in the animal trade, capturing and selling turtles and other reptiles. Besides almost wiping out some local species, the reptile trade is wrecking forests with the fire that villagers use to corner the animals.

Then China entered the picture. China had been aggressively logging its own forests until the denuded land caused devastating floods. When Chinese ecologists warned against continued logging in flood plains, China turned to Indonesia for lumber, encouraging that country to cut down even more of its forests.

These are the kinds of things that happen in a world where countries and financial institutions pursue their interests without regard to the impact on the earth as a whole. The Indonesian government has been unable or unwilling to stop the relentless logging, even in its national forests. In 2001, the World Bank predicted that, at the current rate, lowland rainforests will become extinct on the island of Sumatra by 2005, and in Borneo soon after 2010. Perhaps the best symbol of this crisis is the orangutan. According to a 2001 study by the Bronx Zoo-based Wildlife Conservation Society, the orangutan—the only great ape found in Asia—may vanish from the wild within a decade unless illegal logging of its habitat and poaching of the species can be greatly reduced.

is that no one can possibly know the impact of all the changes we are making. Can we do without all of those species that were lost last year? What exactly will happen in our oceans if we destroy all the coral reefs? How little rainforest can we get by with? We have to ask ourselves if we really want to carry out all these experiments on our planet. Right now there are too many people performing too many actions that have too many unknown consequences.

Humanity needs to slow down and to look more carefully at where it's stepping. To do that, it first needs to ease up on its reproductive rate and to back up to a level of population in which there are not so many pressures on people—and entire nations—to do careless and desperate things. Some ecologists have suggested that a sustainable world population may be as low as two billion people—about the number there were in the 1920s. That may sound like too radical a proposal. Given what's happening in the world right now, however, it's hard to make a case that six billion or anything higher is a sustainable level.

Many problems remain to be solved in the world. Limiting population will by no means completely solve all of them. Even a world of many fewer people can have environmental problems. An affluent, high-tech society of superconsumers, for example, could continue to pollute, or chop down too much forest, or be wasteful with water. We've already seen how the richest one billion people of today's world consume such a disproportionate share of the world's resources and contribute disproportionately to many environmental problems.

Nevertheless, reducing, or at least stabilizing population would ease the pressure on the Earth and give the nations of the world—especially those experiencing runaway growth—some breathing room to work on the problems.

A NEED FOR MORE OPENNESS

It's hard to trust in the wisdom of a world on a subject that it almost completely avoids. People need to begin talking more openly and honestly about population. We saw in Chapter One that there were a host of reasons that people ignored or played down the population problem, from associations with abortion to fears of causing economic problems. We need to stop worrying so much about bringing up a difficult subject, or whether overpopulation and its solutions seem "too negative." There *are* negative aspects to the situation. Ask the people who are living in the shantytowns, or the migrants who allow themselves to be sealed into steel containers in hope of reaching a better place, or the fisherman whose livelihood has disappeared, or anyone who lives on a coastline and is wondering where that coastline will be in twenty years.

Nor is it a solution to face each one of these problems individually as if they weren't related. Even many environmentalists steer clear of overpopulation, focusing instead on carefully defined causes such as "saving the rainforest" or "endangered animals" so as not to alienate supporters. We need to connect the dots and to acknowledge the role of population in these problems. There's a saying among some environmentalists that "Whatever your cause, it's a lost cause—unless we come to grips with overpopulation."

CHANGING OUR WAYS

Human society today remains divided into two demographic worlds, and each has a different aspect of the population problem to solve.

The challenge in the less developed countries—where 95 percent of future population growth will occur—is to continue lowering fertility. In sub-Saharan Africa, for example, women are still having an average of four children each. As population continues to swell in these societies, the world is going to see more of the problems of those societies: malnutrition and hunger, poor sanitation and infectious diseases, shantytowns and homelessness, joblessness and poverty, migration and border wars. By 2050, 90 percent of the world's population will be in what are today considered the less developed countries.

On the other side of the divide are the industrialized countries. They have lowered their birth rates but must now find ways to reduce their destructive impact on the environment, and to strive for a more equitable distribution of food and resources. To prevent further buildup of greenhouse gases, they need to find and use alternative energy sources. People may have to learn to live more simply, consuming less meat, driving less, and living in smaller homes.

The world may have held together so far because only a little more than a billion of the world's people are superconsumers. But what happens when the rest of the world catches up to them. Can the world sustain nine or ten billion superconsumers?

WHAT CAN YOU DO?

The most important thing you can do is to be informed, to read about the population problem, and to discuss environmental problems with your teachers, friends, and parents. Many otherwise informed people know very little about population problems because so little appears in the media. Study the publications of such organizations as Zero Population Growth. If you agree with a group's goals, you can subscribe to its newsletter, make a donation, or offer your services as a volunteer. You can also write letters to your government representatives to see where they stand on the issue of family planning and international birth control programs, and you can tell them your views. Study the articles in your local newspaper about environmental and resource related articles to see if they mention overpopulation. If not, write letters to the editor, pointing out the connection.

The organizations listed in the Appendix can provide you with more information about overpopulation, population and the environment, and population control.

Glossary

aquaculture the cultivation of water plants and animals for human use or consumption; fish-farming.

aquifers underground formations of porous rock that hold groundwater.

biodiversity the variety of organisms found within a particular area or region.

birth control practices employed by couples that permit sexual intercourse with reduced chance of conception. The term birth control is often used synonymously with such terms as contraception, fertility control, and family planning.

birth rate the number of people born each year for every thousand people in a given population.

carrying capacity the number of inhabitants—plants or animals—that a particular area can support over a long period of time without any environmental harm to that region or habitat.

census an official count of a population which usually includes information about people such as their sex, age, income, and other facts.

death rate the number of people who die every year out of every thousand people in a given population.

demographer a person who studies human population and such characteristics as size, growth, birth and death rates, and global distribution.

demographics   the statistical characteristics of a given population.

demographic transition   the downward shift of birth and death rates in a population according to a historical pattern. In this pattern the death rate goes down first, causing more children to live, and then the birth rate goes down. The result is a stable or slow-growing population.

demography   the study of population size, density, and distribution.

doubling time   the length of time it takes for a population to double in size.

ecosystem   a community of plants, animals, and microscopic organisms interacting with each other and their environment.

exponential growth   increasing in extraordinary proportions because of a greatly increased base population. Exponential growth starts slowly, but after a time grows very rapidly.

family planning   the conscious effort of couples to regulate the number and spacing of births through the use of contraception.

fertility rate   the average number of children that a woman in a population will have if the birth rate remains the same.

fossil fuels   coal, oil (petroleum), and natural gas, which were formed from the fossilized remains of ancient plants and other organisms. When fossil fuels are burned, they give off carbon dioxide.

global warming   the gradual increase in the planet's temperature that is believed to be caused by a combination of natural cycles and the accumulation of human-produced greenhouse gases in the atmosphere.

graying population   a group of people, such as a nation, in which the largest proportion are middle-aged and older.

growth rate   the rate at which a population is increasing (or decreasing) in a given year due to natural increase and migration, expressed as a percentage of the base population. Also called the *rate of natural increase.*

infant mortality rate   the number of children who die before reaching one year of age for every thousand births.

life expectancy   the average number of years that a newborn infant in a particular population can be expected to live, if the *death rate* doesn't change.

monoculture   an agriculture based on a single plant variety or strain.

nonrenewable resource   natural resources such as water, topsoil, minerals, or metals formed by geologic processes that take thousands to millions of years.

overfishing   taking so many fish from a lake, river, or ocean that there are not enough reproductive stock left to replenish them.

pandemic   a worldwide epidemic.

population density   the number of people living in a square mile or a square kilometer.

population density map   a diagram showing the concentrations of people in a specific region.

population momentum   the tendency of a population to keep growing beyond the time that replacement rate has been reached, because of a relatively high concentration of people in the childbearing years.

replacement rate   the number of children it takes to maintain the population at the same level. This is usually slightly more than two because of infant mortality.

subsistence level   the minimal amount of food, water, and other necessities required to keep a human being alive.

sustainable population   a population that doesn't have a destructive impact on the Earth and one that doesn't reduce the capacity of the Earth to support future generations.

technological optimism   the confident belief that technology and human know-how can solve future problems, specifically problems caused by environmental abuse and resource depletion.

technological skepticism   the belief that some problems may be beyond the ability of human technology to solve.

zero population growth   a stable population, one that is neither growing nor shrinking.

To Find Out More

BOOKS

Brown, Lester, Gary Gardner, and Brian Halweil. *Beyond Malthus: Nineteen Dimensions of the Population Challenge.* New York: W.W. Norton, 1999.

Ehrlich, Paul. *The Population Explosion.* New York: Simon & Schuster, 1990.

Gallant, Roy A. *The Peopling of the Planet Earth: Human Population Growth Through the Ages.* New York: Macmillan, 1990.

Giblin, James Cross. *When Plague Strikes: The Black Death, Smallpox, AIDS.* New York: HarperCollins, 1995.

Lappe, Frances Moore. *Diet for a Small Planet.* New York: Ballantine, 1982.

Lomborg, Bjorn. *The Skeptical Environmentalist: Measuring the Real State of the World.* Cambridge, U.K. Cambridge University Press, 2001.

McKibben, Bill. *Maybe One: A Personal and Environmental Argument for Single Child Families.* New York: Simon & Schuster, 1998.

Meyers, Norman and Julian Simon. *Scarcity or Abundance? A Debate on the Environment.* New York: W.W. Norton, 1994.

Preston, Richard. *The Hot Zone.* New York: Random House, 1994.

Stefoff, Rebecca. *Overpopulation.* New York: Chelsea House, 1993.

REPORTS AND PUBLICATIONS

Gelbard, Alene, Carl Haub, and Mary M. Kent. *World Population Beyond Six Billion.* Population Reference Bureau, 1999.

Haub, Carl, and Diana Cornelius. *The Century of Population.* Population Reference Bureau, 1999.

Livermash, Robert, and Eric Rodenburg. *Population Change, Resources, and the Environment.* Population Reference Bureau, 1998.

United Nations Population Division. *The World at Six Billion.* October 1999.

ORGANIZATIONS AND WEB SITES

Population Council
One Dag Hammarskjold Plaza
New York, NY 10017
(212) 339-0500
www.popcouncil.org

Population Institute
107 Second Street, NE
Washington, DC 20002
(800) 787-0038
www.populationinstitute.org

Population Reference Bureau, Inc.
1875 Connecticut Avenue
Suite 520
Washington, DC 20009-5728
(202) 483-1100
www.prb.org

United Nations Population Fund (UNFPA)
220 East 42nd Street
New York, NY 10017
www.unfpa.org

United Nations Population Information Network (POPIN)
www.un.org/popin

U.S. Census Bureau
Washington, DC 20233
(301) 457-4608
www.census.gov

Worldwatch Institute
1776 Massachusetts Avenue, NW
Washington, DC 20036-1904
(202) 452-1999
www.worldwatch.org

Zero Population Growth
1400 Sixteenth Street, NW
Suite 320
Washington, DC 20036
(202) 332-2200
www.zpg.org

Index